JUMPSTART!
SCIENCE OUTDOORS

This collection of engaging and simple-to-use activities will jumpstart students' understanding of science by taking teaching and learning outdoors and linking it to a specific area of the curriculum.

A wealth of practical activities in the book covers all areas – from identifying, classifying and grouping to pattern seeking, making observations and comparative and fair testing.

This cross-curricular approach encourages teachers to develop useful links with other subjects that support and complement the science. With links to a range of online resources and more than 40 motivating and engaging science activities, cross-curricular links cover the following areas of the curriculum:

- maths, English, computing, history, geography, music, art, PE, RE, PSHE and design and technology.

Jumpstart! Science Outdoors is an essential classroom resource that will encourage the personal development of children and is the perfect solution for helping teachers, teaching assistants and students deliver effective and imaginative science lessons.

Janet Barnett is an experienced, award-winning primary teacher and science specialist. She is a Chartered Science Teacher and a Fellow of the Primary Science Teacher College, UK.

Rosemary Feasey is a leading expert in primary science with experience across the primary age range in the classroom. She is a freelance science consultant and author of a wide range of materials.

Jumpstart!

Jumpstart! Grammar (2nd Edition)
Games and activities for ages 6–14
Pie Corbett and Julia Strong

Jumpstart! Talk for Learning
Games and activities for ages 7–12
John Foster and Lyn Dawes

Jumpstart! PSHE
Games and activities for ages 7–13
John Foster

Jumpstart! History
Engaging activities for ages 7–12
*Sarah Whitehouse and
Karen Vickers-Hulse*

Jumpstart! Geography
Engaging activities for ages 7–12
Sarah Whitehouse and Mark Jones

**Jumpstart! Thinking Skills and
Problem Solving**
Games and activities for ages 7–14
Steve Bowkett

Jumpstart! Maths (2nd Edition)
Maths activities and games for
ages 5–14
John Taylor

Jumpstart! Spanish and Italian
Engaging activities for ages 7–12
Catherine Watts and Hilary Phillips

Jumpstart! French and German
Engaging activities for ages 7–12
Catherine Watts and Hilary Phillips

Jumpstart! Drama
Games and activities for ages 5–11
*Teresa Cremin, Roger McDonald,
Emma Goff and Louise Blakemore*

Jumpstart! Science
Games and activities for ages 5–11
Rosemary Feasey

Jumpstart! Storymaking
Games and activities for ages 7–12
Pie Corbett

Jumpstart! Poetry
Games and activities for ages 7–12
Pie Corbett

Jumpstart! Creativity
Games and activities for ages 7–14
Steve Bowkett

Jumpstart! ICT
ICT activities and games for
ages 7–14
John Taylor

Jumpstart! Numeracy
Maths activities and games for
ages 5–14
John Taylor

Jumpstart! Literacy
Key Stage 2/3 literacy games
Pie Corbett

JUMPSTART! SCIENCE OUTDOORS

CROSS-CURRICULAR GAMES AND
ACTIVITIES FOR AGES 5–12

Janet Barnett and Rosemary Feasey

Routledge
Taylor & Francis Group

LONDON AND NEW YORK

First published 2016
by Routledge
2 Park Square, Milton Park, Abingdon, Oxon OX14 4RN

and by Routledge
711 Third Avenue, New York, NY 10017

Routledge is an imprint of the Taylor & Francis Group, an informa business

British Library Cataloguing in Publication Data
A catalogue record for this book is available from the British Library

Library of Congress Cataloging in Publication Data
Names: Barnett, Janet, author. | Feasey, Rosemary, author. Title: Jumpstart! science outdoors : cross-curricular games and activities for ages 5-12 / Janet Barnett and Rosemary Feasey.Description: Abingdon, Oxon ; New York, NY : Routledge, 2016.Identifiers: LCCN 2015032849 | ISBN 9781138925052 (hbk.) | ISBN 9781138925069 (pbk.) | ISBN 9781315683997 (ebk.) Subjects: LCSH: Science--Study and teaching (Secondary)--Activity programs. | Natural history--Study and teaching (Secondary)--Activity programs. Classification: LCC Q181 .B323 2016 | DDC 507.1/2--dc23LC record available at http://lccn.loc.gov/2015032849

ISBN: 978-1-138-92505-2 (hbk)
ISBN: 978-1-138-92506-9 (pbk)
ISBN: 978-1-315-68399-7 (ebk)

Typeset in Palatino and Scala Sans
by Saxon Graphics Ltd, Derby

To Ray, Rosa and Gregory at 'Home Sweet Home'.

Janet

To my Mum who is simply the best.

Rosemary

Contents

Acknowledgements

To all those teachers and children who, over the years, have shared their ideas and inspired us both.

Illustrations based on original drawings by Simone Hesketh.

Introduction

Jumpstart! Science Outdoors provides teachers with a range of lively, short, fun activities and games to support teaching and learning using different aspects of the science curriculum outdoors in the school grounds or local environment. What makes this book unique is that, for each activity, the teacher is provided with the most relevant links to other areas of the curriculum.

WHY OUTDOORS?

Schools are moving rapidly towards teachers and children making decisions about whether learning should take place indoors or outdoors – the expectation being that in science, unless there is a good reason for being indoors, the science should take place in the school grounds or local area. Children prefer working outdoors: they enjoy the freedom the space offers and the fresh air; a change from classrooms, which can be stuffy and cramped. Of course, for most children the outdoors is much more interesting, so motivation is high and children enjoy using the natural and built resources that the outdoors offers.

On a practical note, the school grounds are a rich source of resources from natural and made materials, to light and shadows, sounds, slopes and surfaces, as well as places to explore and design and make. All this saves the teacher time and energy in hunting down and collecting suitable resources when all they have to do in most schools is walk outside where there are sufficient resources for the whole class.

Working outdoors also supports important elements of the science curriculum and scientific enquiry, such as: observation over time; pattern seeking; identifying; and classifying and grouping. The key aims of the activities in this book are to support children in applying their scientific knowledge and understanding as well as thinking and working scientifically. Importantly, the activities are aimed at consolidating and further developing children's achievement in science in a range of contexts. Taking science outside enables children to develop as independent learners, increasing personal skills such as perseverance and working with others.

WHO IS THE BOOK FOR?

Jumpstart! Science Outdoors is for anyone who is looking to take science outdoors. It aims to support both those teachers taking their first steps outside with their class in science, and those who have already moved their science outdoors on a regular basis and are looking for additional interesting activities to extend the scope of the science and add breadth and depth through cross-curricular links.

This book will also be useful to others in your school, so remember to share it with Teaching Assistants (TAs) and Higher Level Teaching Assistants (HLTAs) as well as student teachers so that they understand each activity and can support children appropriately.

WHY LINK WITH OTHER AREAS OF THE CURRICULUM?

Science is not an island to be taught on its own; it needs other subjects such as Mathematics, English and Computing. In fact, science depends on applying number skills, taking measurements and for children to be able to communicate their science confidently in different ways. To this end, science and computing go hand in hand – for example, when children use data loggers to collect temperature or sound readings, or video or photograph aspects of the outdoors (such as seasonal changes in trees) as well as themselves in action.

Science also provides a natural partner for other areas of the curriculum such as history, where children might be testing the roof for an Iron Age hut or art, when they create a sculpture or picture using natural materials.

USING *JUMPSTART! SCIENCE OUTDOORS* EXPLOITS RELATIONSHIPS ACROSS THE CURRICULUM

There are more than 40 engaging activities in this book. All activities are practical, easy-to-do and highly motivating for both teachers and children. Here are some suggestions for using this book.

- Look through the book from different perspectives; you may begin with science but if you are looking for an outdoor history or RE activity, check out the cross-curricular links to help you find an activity.
- Allocate time for each activity; don't be tempted to rush through activities, otherwise the children will be less likely to fully benefit.
- Use the activities on a regular basis rather than as one-off sessions so that children can develop as independent learners and become familiar with expectations for behaviour and working practices when outdoors.
- Activities are meant to support collaborative working, so children working in groups of two, three and four is ideal.
- Allocate one person in each group as the Resource Manager who has to make sure that all resources taken out are returned; you might even invest in a set of cheap haversacks to carry resources.

The activities can be used:

- as a starting point for a science topic
- as a regular part of your science schemes of work
- as part of a cross-curricular topic
- to develop fieldwork skills
- for a science or gardening club.

Jumpstart! Science Outdoors exploits relationships across the curriculum, encouraging teachers to develop creative approaches to motivating and engaging children in science outdoors. Each activity is structured to indicate the:

* science knowledge and understanding
* type of enquiry activity
* resources
* relevant cross-curricular activity.

HEALTH AND SAFETY OUTDOORS

Science outdoors is no different from mathematics, physical education or geography outdoors, or indeed playtime outdoors, since all of these should be covered by your generic school outdoors policy. There are few issues relating to safety in Primary Science; safety is highlighted in activities where appropriate. If you are unsure please read *ASE Be Safe!*, which is published by the Association for Science Education (more details can be obtained from www.ase.org.uk).

Alternatively, find out if your school or LA is a member of CLEAPSS which also provides safety information for primary science www.cleapss.org.uk.

Forest Schools
If you are a Forest School you will recognise that the activities in this book encourage children to develop their relationship with the natural world around them. Key to many activities is encouraging children to make sense of and use the school grounds, in particular using some of the skills and understanding they have developed during Forest School experiences. This means that the most obvious approach to take with children who have these experiences is to encourage them to work independently, take risks in their thinking and use the resources in the school grounds to solve problems. In this way, children will deepen their understanding and appreciation of their immediate outdoor environment.

Adopt a tree

Saying 'hello' to your tree

Science topics
Plants; Seasonal change

Activity type
Observation over time

Resources
Audio equipment, e.g. Talk Tins, Easi Speak microphones

Cameras

Pencils

Sketchbooks

Video

Overview
The aim of this activity is to develop children's understanding of a single tree through observation across several years, so that children begin to understand how a tree changes over time and that its seasonal cycle is repeated each year.

ACTIVITY

- Discuss with children the idea of adopting a tree and finding out as much as they can about it by observing it regularly, e.g. every two weeks, once a month or as often as they want. Take the children outside to look at one or more trees, and to think about what they could find out and observe over time. They could write or have scribed their ideas using chalks on the playground or on a wall. Ask for ideas about how they could keep a record of their observations, e.g. photographs, sketches, notebook, video, audio recording. You could pre-empt their ideas by making a collection and placing them in a box for children to choose from so that they can begin to record on their first visit.

- Take children to a tree and ask them to think about which parts of the tree they can name, e.g. trunk, canopy, roots, twigs, branches, leaves, seeds, flowers, bark. Challenge them to remember the name of any part that they did not already know.

- Working in groups, children choose and adopt a tree in the school grounds. Send them off to 'say hello' to their tree and give it a hug to find out what it feels like, its texture and size compared to themselves. What does it smell like? If they stand still what can they hear, e.g. leaves rustling? How many different things can they find out about their tree in, say, 5 or 10 minutes?

- Once children have had time to find out about their tree ask them to record interesting things using video, taking photos, sketching, etc. For example, they could take photographs of their tree from different angles and of different parts, e.g. bark, leaves, trunk and canopy.

- Depending on the ability of the children, give them a sketchbook and pencil to sketch the shape of their tree, concentrating on whether it is tall, short, wide, narrow, oval, circular, heart shaped.

- They could also use their sketchbook to take a bark rubbing and a leaf rubbing.

- Finally, give children tree identification sheets, books or cards to use to find out the name of their tree.

SCIENCE BACKGROUND

Many school grounds have trees which provide opportunities for children not only to develop their understanding of a plant and its life cycle but also of classification, habitats and food chains. Importantly, when children study trees they can do so over one or more years, developing concepts of change over time, seasonal change and life cycles. When a child adopts a tree and explores it each year using their increasing subject knowledge and skills, they deepen and broaden their understanding so that the child becomes an expert.

CROSS-CURRICULAR LINKS

English
Children use discussion about their 'adopted' tree to decide how to record what they find out and how to share ideas about what the tree looks, feels and sounds like, etc. Challenge children to use scientific terminology relating to trees, e.g. trunk, canopy, bark, roots as well as mathematical language, e.g. shape, size. Children could keep a tree journal and include regular photographs of themselves next to their adopted tree so that they can see how both change during their school years.

Computing
Children use the world of digital technology to choose how to record what they find out about their tree according to their ability and interest. They should be able to discuss and select which media they want to use and their reasons for their choices, e.g. camera, video, audio, and then review how well they think the approach worked.

Online resources
www.nhm.ac.uk/take-part/identify-nature.html

Adopt a tree

Exploring leaves

Science topic
Plants

Activity type
Observation over time

Resources
Binoculars

Cameras

Magnifying lenses

Pencils

Sketchbooks

Video

Overview
The aim of this activity is to develop children's understanding of their adopted tree through close observation of tree leaves.

ACTIVITY

Children return to their adopted tree and explore the tree's leaves. Ask them what they will look for when observing the leaves. They may suggest the following.

- **Shape:** Leaf shapes are divided into groups: needle-like, simple (one leaf), palmate (the leaflets join to a central point, sometimes looking like hands like those seen on horse chestnut) or pinnate (where the leaflets are opposite each other with one leaflet at the top).
- **Leaf edges:** Trees can be identified by the leaf edges – for example, some are lobed like ear lobes such as oak; others are tooth-like such as silver birch or spiky like holly.
- **Colour:** There are many shades of green, and children can develop their understanding of this by collecting a range of leaves to see how many different shades they can find. Similarly, children could collect and order leaves across one or more colour spectrums such as yellow, through gold to red.
- **Texture:** Leaves do have a texture: some are hairy like some willow tree leaves; others are waxy, e.g. like holly.
- **Arrangement of leaves:** Some leaves are opposite each other on a stem (e.g. maple); others are alternate on a stem (such as willow).

Encourage children to use magnifying lenses to enhance their observations as well as binoculars for looking up into trees and digital cameras to take photographs or video clips of leaves on trees.

Remind children to return to the adopted tree regularly and observe how the leaves change across the seasons.

While children are outdoors they could:

- create Venn diagrams on the playground using chalks to sort leaves
- sort leaves using frames made from twigs
- sort leaves from darkest to lightest colour
- using leaves of the same colour, sort them from darkest to lightest shade
- sort leaves from widest to narrowest or longest to shortest.

SCIENCE BACKGROUND

Careful observation is essential for identifying and naming trees and is based on children observing key features of leaves – including shape, veins, leaf edges, etc. Part of observing leaves involves developing scientific language to describe their characteristics, e.g. shape, simple, compound. Depending on the ability of children, some might understand that we should try not to pick leaves to observe but to use fallen leaves because trees need leaves to make food.

CROSS-CURRICULAR LINKS

Mathematics
Create leaf-shaped mathematics challenge cards such as the following examples.

- Find the smallest and biggest leaf, narrowest and widest leaf.
- How can you find out the area of the largest and smallest leaf from your 'adopted' tree?
- What is the average area of the leaves on your 'adopted' tree?
- What is the average size leaf on your 'adopted' tree?

Art
Children use a range of art techniques:

- **Collage** to create woodland animals made from leaves, for example, beetles, owls and mice around their 'adopted tree', taking photographs and video clips of their work.
- **Clay leaves** where children roll out and press a leaf into the clay, cutting round the leaf shape. Once dried, the clay can be painted and varnished. If a hole is made before drying, the leaf could be hung using string, once finished.
- **Leaf prints** using paint and creating pictures of repeated patterns.
- **Leaf rubbings** using crayons then cutting the leaves out to add to a class display picture of showing the tree that season.

Online resources
www.nhm.ac.uk/take-part/identify-nature.html

Adopt a tree

How much can you find out about the tree bark?

Science topics
Plants; Seasonal change

Activity type
Observing over time

Resources
Cameras

Paper and pencils

Sketchbooks

Video

Overview
The aim of this activity is to further develop children's understanding of their adopted tree through close observation of its bark.

ACTIVITY

Children return to their adopted tree and explore the bark on the tree trunk. Ask them what they will look for when observing bark. They may suggest the following.

- **Colour:** Bark colour varies from white and silver, to reds and browns. For example, silver birch has a silvery white bark which sheds layers like tissue paper and becomes black and rugged at the base. As the trees mature, the bark develops dark, diamond-shaped fissures.

- **Texture:** Not all tree bark feels the same. Some barks are silky; others bumpy. Beech trees have a smooth bark, while the bark of oak trees starts off smooth but, as they age, becomes rugged with cracks and crevices.
- **Pattern:** This varies. Some have horizontal ridges while others are vertical. Other trees have dashes on them (e.g. silver birch) while the bark of some trees looks like a jigsaw. Many have diagonal stripes or spots on them.
- **Animals:** Bark provides a habitat for many animals (especially invertebrates) which in turn provides food for a range of birds.
- **Damage:** Children should observe the bark to see if it is rubbed, torn, stripped off, burrowed through or looks diseased.

SCIENCE BACKGROUND

The bark of a tree is like the skin of a human; its function is to protect the tree trunk from damage and drying out. If the bark is damaged, the tree will ooze sap which will then harden to protect where the tree has been damaged. When human skin is damaged, it can become infected; when tree bark is damaged, fungi and disease can get in and affect the tree's health. Some bark is used for commercial purposes, e.g. cork, and for the production of drugs for conditions such as arthritis. Tannin found in bark from oak trees has been used to tan leather since Roman times.

CROSS-CURRICULAR LINKS

English
Children ask a range of questions about bark prior to going back to their adopted tree using a range of question stems, e.g. What does it feel like? Which animals live on the bark? Where are there cracks? They try to answer their questions through observing the bark, taking rubbings, looking for damage and invertebrates. Where children are unable to take practical action to find an answer, they

can research the information using secondary sources such as finding information about moss or lichen growing on tree bark using books or searching online. Children can create a mini bark book to record and share what they have found out. The cover could even be made from a sheet of paper decorated with bark rubbings taken from their tree.

Art

Children sketch bark using charcoal or use different fabrics, string and wool to create bark patterns and textures. Display this work in a Tree Gallery as part of a class or whole school exhibition on trees. Children use their own bark rubbings to create a 'bark' trail around the school grounds for other children to follow, and find which bark matches which tree. This trail could also include QR codes linking to websites with further information about each tree type.

Online resources

www.nhm.ac.uk/take-part/identify-nature.html

ACTIVITY 4
Mini collections

Science topic
Plants and animals

Activity type
Identifying, classifying and grouping

Resources
Small containers, e.g. film canisters, 1 between 2 children

Overview

Children collect items from outdoors and use them to classify into different groups; they also identify and name what they have collected. The children use a film canister so that only small objects or materials are taken from the environment, and so that if the work needs to be continued in the classroom, tables are not filled with half of the school grounds. Limiting children also means that they have to observe carefully to find objects and items that fit into the canisters.

ACTIVITY

- Take children outside with their collection pots. Ask them to work with a partner to fill their pot with as many different things as they can find in a given time, e.g. 10 minutes. Explain that they should choose carefully, that they cannot have the same thing twice and that they must be able to put the lid on the canister when they have finished.
- Tell children to find somewhere to sit so they can empty their pot and then work with their partner to sort their collection as many different ways as they can. Children could:

  - sort their collections according to colour, shape, texture, natural/not natural, size, parts of a plant
  - sort in order, e.g. colour (dark to light) or size
  - classify the objects using scientific groups, e.g. seeds, evergreen etc.

- As they are working, visit each group and listen to their ideas and classifications.
- Ask children if they have found any parts of a plant. If they have, could they create a whole plant? Where children do not have all the parts from the same plant, they could use what parts they have to create a 'new plant'.
- Ask children to create a plant life cycle, e.g. leaf, flower, seed, seedling, decaying leaf.
- When they have finished classifying their collection, ask them to identify each item. If they don't know what it is, they should use

an identification sheet or book, or ask children in other groups. Any items they cannot identify could be taken back to class and placed on a 'Can you identify it?' table, and children challenged to use books, the internet or find out from home what it is.

SCIENCE BACKGROUND

In this activity children are grouping, classifying and identifying. Grouping is the process of placing objects into groups, any kind of group of their choice (e.g. colour, shape), whereas classification is arranging items according to scientific terms, e.g. animals, plants, waterproof, deciduous, flower. Identification is giving a name to something, e.g. petal, seed, plastic.

CROSS-CURRICULAR LINKS

English

Working with their partner, children look at the objects from their canister and use as many as possible to tell a story. For example, if they find a pigeon feather, moss, twig and berries from a hedge, their story might be something like this:

A bird was flying over the hedge, spotted berries and flew down to eat some. Then, when it had finished, it spotted some moss and twigs. 'Ah,' it thought, 'I could use those for my nest.' So it flew down and tried to collect both with its beak. It was so busy doing this that it did not see the cat, who pounced, caught the bird and dragged it off, leaving only a feather behind.

Children could take a photo of their collection and write their story for a class story book or use an Easi Speak microphone to record their story for other children to listen to alongside a photograph.

Art

Using the items collected in their canisters, children create an outdoor 'environmental art' picture or sculpture and photograph it once completed so they have a record. Ask children: How do you think the artwork will change over the next few days? Which factors might cause these changes? (Examples include wind, rain, animals, humans.) You could show children photos of Andy Goldsworthy's work prior to this activity, explaining that he photographs his sculptures and leaves his work outdoors, sometimes returning to watch it change and decay. Children could return to their environmental art each day and photograph the changes.

ACTIVITY 5

Nature's viewing frame

Science topics
Living things and their habitat; Seasonal change

Activity type
Observation over time

Resources
Optional camera

Seasonal change diary

String

Twigs

Viewing frame

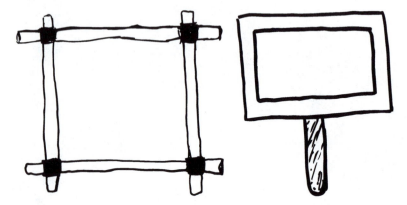

Overview

The aim of this activity is for children to create a 'viewing frame' (see the illustrations above) using, e.g., twigs with string, Lego® or card, and then choosing a place in the school grounds to observe regularly across the school year. Children sketch or photograph what they observe through their viewing frames, recording their observations in their personal seasonal change diary or on a calendar.

ACTIVITY

- Children make their viewing frame using, e.g. twigs and string, and practise looking through the frame to view different areas around the school grounds.
- What can children see? How many different plants and animals can they find? Which ones can they identify and name? Challenge children to focus on the detail of what is in the frame, e.g.:

  - number
  - name
  - shape
  - colours
  - size
  - texture.

- Ask children to take a formal photograph of the area they can see through their view or to sketch what they see.
- Once children are familiar with how their viewing frame can be used, ask them to adopt an area of the school grounds that they think would be interesting to observe throughout the year. Tell children that, whichever view they choose, they will return to it regularly – e.g. fortnightly for the rest of the year – so that they can observe how the area changes through the seasons.
- The first sketch or photograph they make of their chosen view should be detailed, because all the other pictures will be compared with this one.
- Children keep a record of their photographs or sketches in a seasonal change diary or a special seasonal calendar.

- Children use their diary or calendar to reflect on previous photographs or sketches, and list the things that have stayed the same and what has changed.
- Ask children to identify the biggest change, and think about what caused the change.
- Focus children's observations on key features – e.g. which colours have changed – and record using coloured pencils or paint sample cards. Children could create colour swatches illustrating the different colours, e.g. in the sky, grass, leaves. This can be used to compare colours across the year and discuss colour changes through the seasons.
- Children could also record the weather conditions on the day they used their viewer, e.g. wind strength and direction, temperature, precipitation.

SCIENCE BACKGROUND

Children need to observe change over time, which means that they require access to the outdoors environment on a regular basis. Using a viewing frame helps to focus children's attention on the same area throughout the year and they can record what they observe. Using their records, they can refer back to previous viewings and compare similarities and differences, noting a range of changes, describing and also explaining what caused them, according to their subject knowledge.

The viewers could be displayed with a photograph or sketch of their observations fastened to the viewer and placed on the wall or a table.

CROSS-CURRICULAR LINKS

English
Different aspects of literacy can be developed from this set of activities. Children are given the freedom and responsibility to observe and record what they see through their viewer across the

year, and communicate their observations. Each time children use the viewer, offer them a different way of recording their observations. Inspire them to use rich descriptive language alongside scientific vocabulary, celebrating the changes that take place across the year. Children should be encouraged to use the language of comparison, such as: compare, similarities, differences, same, different, cause, effect, result.

Art

Children design and make a viewing frame and sketch or draw what they observe, thinking about colour, pattern, texture, line, shape, form and space. Children will benefit from lessons teaching them how to sketch, so that they can confidently use their sketchbooks to record their observations. They should also be encouraged to review observations with the aim to improve their mastery of drawing and sketching.

Amazing seed dispersal

Science topics
Living things and their habitat; Seed dispersal

Activity type
Identifying, classifying and grouping

Resources
Camera

Clipboards

Magnifying lens

Pencils

Sketchbook

Tree and flower identification keys

Video camera

Overview
This activity provides children with opportunities to find, explore and identify seeds across the seasons.

ACTIVITY

- During spring, summer and autumn, make regular visits outdoors to find plants that are producing seeds – regular visits across the seasons because different plants produce their seeds at different times of the year.
- It is useful to have done some work on seed dispersal prior to going outside so that children know some of the main methods of dispersal, which might include video clips showing seed dispersal in slow motion (see Online resources).
- Tell children that they are going to survey the school grounds to find out how many different kinds of seed dispersal they can find and also identify and name the plants. Children should have access to, and use, identification charts and books for this aspect.
- If children have an outdoors fieldwork sketchbook they can sketch the plant and the method of seed dispersal, annotating their sketch. Magnifying lenses are very useful here for children to carry out close observations of the dispersal mechanism to help their sketching.
- Of course, children could collect their results and place them on a table or chart chalked on the school playground or walls, sharing their results with other children.
- Once they have completed collecting their data, they should analyse it and draw conclusions about the type of plants and seed dispersal in their school grounds.

SCIENCE BACKGROUND

To grow, seeds need sunlight, air, nutrition and water; if they are too close to the parent plant then there is competition for these resources. Plants have developed amazing ways to send their seedlings away so that they can germinate successfully, e.g. wind (such as parachutes like dandelions and willowherb); wings (such as sycamore seeds and cedar); and shaking (poppy, love in the mist), which works like a pepper pot and scatters seeds in the wind.

Other methods include these:

- **Water:** Seeds such as coconut float across seas; alder seeds can float long distances.
- **Drop and roll:** Horse chestnuts, drop, roll away and the case splits open revealing the seed (conker); oak.
- **Bursting (explosion):** Seeds are flung away, e.g. peas and Himalayan Balsam.
- **Animals:** Blackberries, rose hips and holly berries are shiny and brightly coloured to attract birds; they eat the fruit, but the seed inside passes through the bird in its droppings. Acorns from the oak tree are collected and hidden by squirrels and jays; fortunately not all are eaten because the animals forget where some have been hidden. Other seeds are ripped off the plant by birds; sparrows and goldfinches will eat bulrush and thistle seeds.
- **Animals, hitching a lift:** Some plants, e.g. burdock and cleavers, have hooks which catch onto animals (including humans) and are dropped away from the parent plant.

CROSS-CURRICULAR LINKS

PSHE

Challenge children to think of as many reasons as possible why plants are important to humans. What are their thoughts on plants? For example, do they like or dislike them? Maybe they're not bothered or have never thought about them? Children could survey other classes, collate data and then analyse and reflect on their findings.

What suggestions do children have for encouraging other people in the school to observe and find out about plants? How could they develop the school grounds to include many different kinds of plants? Could they design planting areas from around the world – e.g. Mediterranean garden, Alpine garden – and look at how those plants reproduce? How about a wildflower area?

Computing

This activity has the potential for a range of areas of the computing curriculum to be applied to support the science. For example, children could go online and research additional material about seed dispersal, which demands that children work to e-safety guidelines. They could log and handle data, consider multimedia such as watching a YouTube video to explain a kind of seed dispersal, or create their own video clip of, for example, dandelion seeds being blown away.

Online resources

www.gettyimages.co.uk/detail/video/high-speed-exploding-himalayan-balsam-pods-stock-video-footage/143278385

Modelling seed dispersal

Science topics
Living things and their habitat; Seed dispersal

Activity type
Comparative and fair testing

Resources
Camera

Recyclable materials

Sketchbook

Tree and flower identification keys

Video camera

Overview
In this activity children create model seeds – either indoors or outdoors – and then test them to find out how well they replicate the original seed and how it is dispersed.

ACTIVITY

- There are many different ways for children to model seed dispersal. The most creative, and one which enables children to apply their understanding of the mechanics of seed dispersal, is where children are challenged to design and make a model of a seed.

- Give children the opportunity to hunt in the school grounds for different types of seeds and then choose which type of seed they want to design and make.
- Give children access to hand lenses or microscopes so that they can look at how the plant disperses the seed. They could also use their experience from the previous activity 'Amazing seed dispersal' to inform their designs.
- Before designing their model, encourage children to create a magnified drawing of what they see and annotate their drawing so they can work out the different parts and describe or explain how the seeds are dispersed.
- Next, children apply their understanding to design and make their own version of the seed using a range of recyclable materials.
- Where children make seeds such as dandelion seeds, poppy heads and sycamore seeds, they should be challenged to test their design to see how successful it is. This could be done by carrying out a comparative test or a fair test with the original seed.
- Alternatively, children could make seeds to model Greater Burdock, commonly known as 'Sticky Jacks', e.g. a table tennis ball with the hook part of Velcro® stuck on.
- For seeds that explode, filling a balloon with confetti or paper bits from a hole-puncher and then bursting it with a pin works well. In this activity exploding the balloon on the playground and marking the distance the seeds disperse can lead to questions such as: 'How does the size of the balloon affect dispersal?'; and 'How do the number of seeds affect dispersal?'

SCIENCE BACKGROUND

Plants need to disperse seeds away from themselves. Most seeds are produced within a fruit and these fruits disperse seeds in a variety of ways, as explained in the previous activity 'Amazing seed dispersal'. The different types of seed dispersal all have one thing in common: they are designed to ensure that as many seeds as possible have a good chance of growing up to produce seeds of their own. If seedlings fell close to the parent plant they would be in competition with the parent; its leaf canopy and root system can spread a good distance, denying the seedling enough light, water and nutrition to grow successfully. This is why plants have dispersal systems to send the seeds as far from the parent as possible.

CROSS-CURRICULAR LINKS

English
Children could write a postcard from a seed telling of its travels; how it got to its final destination and whether it is now in the right environment to grow successfully so that it can be pollinated and produce and disperse its own seeds. On the front of the postcard, children could sketch or draw how the seed is dispersed, or they could sketch the habitat where it has germinated, showing the new plant with seeds.

Design and technology
In this activity children are engaged in a practical and creative challenge which demands that they use their knowledge and understanding of seed dispersal with the process of designing and making a seed. This should be an iterative process where children decide on their design criteria, e.g. make a fruit to disperse seeds and continually test it against the original plant and revise where necessary. When making their design, children should be able to think about the properties of the materials and select those appropriate to their seed. This might also require them to use some technical knowledge. Finally, children should evaluate their seed against those from the plant, asking questions such as: How similar and different is it? Can it be dispersed successfully? How could it be improved?

Online resources
www.bbc.co.uk/education/clips/znvfb9q

www.gettyimages.co.uk/detail/video/high-speed-exploding-himalayan-balsam-pods-stock-video-footage/143278385

www.saps.org.uk/primary/teaching-resources/200-designing-a-seed

ACTIVITY 8
Prickly holly

Science topics
Plants; Living things in their habitat

Activity type
Pattern seeking

Resources
Chalk

Plastic trays to collect holly leaves

⚠ **Safety: Many schools have holly in their grounds; it can safely be handled by children but remember it is a poisonous plant. The berries must never be eaten; the leaves can also be toxic so make sure children wash their hands after use.**

Overview
In this activity children explore the plant holly to find out about it, and then carry out data-handling and pattern-seeking activities using holly leaves they have collected.

ACTIVITY

- Give children time to explore and get to know the holly tree or bush in the school grounds (or perhaps the local park), and to work with a partner or in a small group to find out as much as they can about this plant, e.g. height, width, colour, berries.

- Children could use chalk on the playground or on a wall on the school building to draw large holly leaves and place a fact about the holly inside each leaf. This then becomes a working wall of information gathered by children to share what they have found out.
- As children are working, prompt closer observation by asking a range of 'I wonder ...?' questions such as, 'I wonder ...

    - ... if all holly leaves are the same colour?'
    - ... if all holly leaves are the same size?'
    - ... if all holly leaves have prickles?'
    - ... what has made the marks on some holly leaves?'

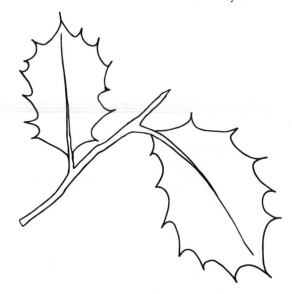

- When children have explored and gathered information about the holly, ask them to collect 10 holly leaves per group. Each individual group classifies them in as many ways as they can, e.g. shades of green, length, width, prickles or no prickles, number of prickles, marks on the leaves, etc.
- Then challenge the children to think about mathematical questions that they would like to find the answers to. They might ask, or be prompted to ask, 'I wonder ...

- ... if all holly leaves have the same number of prickles?'
- ... if the number of prickles are always the same on each side of the leaf?'
- ... if longer holly leaves have more prickles?'
- ... if the leaves at the bottom of the holly bush or tree are the same as the ones at the top?'

- To answer these questions, children need to think about how many leaves they would need so that their evidence would be believable. You could introduce the idea of sample size here; would a sample size of 1 be good, for example, to say that all holly leaves have the same number of prickles? What do they think would be a good sample size so that other people would feel confident that their answer was believable?
- Since every group has already collected 10 holly leaves each, children could join with another group or join together as a whole class to count and measure to collect data and look at patterns that emerge to answer their question. Their answer could be placed with their question inside a holly leaf drawn on their outdoor working wall.
- Children could also use their leaves to create a playground surface scattergram (see maths activity below).

SCIENCE BACKGROUND

Common holly is a hardy evergreen tree or shrub with glossy, spiky leaves. The spikes are an adaptation which discourage animals from eating the leaves and also protect birds that eat the berries from predators. Interestingly, leaves on the higher branches have no spikes because few animals can reach to eat them. Some holly trees have variegated leaves which are green with white patches. Holly is dioecious, which means that male and female flowers occur on different trees, so holly flowers need to be pollinated by insects such as bees; when this happens, the flowers develop into the bright red berries that are seen in the autumn and winter. Birds eat the berries and the seeds are dispersed in bird droppings.

CROSS-CURRICULAR LINKS

Mathematics

Children work outdoors and use 'live' data (i.e. holly leaves) to create graphs and draw conclusions from data, e.g. whether all holly leaves have the same number of prickles. On the playground, draw graph axes: number of prickles 1–10 on the horizontal axis; and number of holly leaves on the vertical axis. All children can count the prickles on each holly leaf and physically put the holly leaves on the graph. Alternatively, if it is too windy, children use chalk to draw each holly leaf with the correct number of prickles on the graph.

To answer the question 'Do longer leaves have more prickles?', draw a larger-than-life scatter diagram, with 'number of prickles' on one axis and 'length of leaf' on the other axis so that all children can place their holly leaves in the correct place. Here, the holly leaves take the place of the pencilled dot or cross which they usually plot when they create a paper version. Ask children to look at the scattergram and decide whether they think there is a pattern relating the length of leaf and number of prickles.

History

Holly trees can live up to 300 years. Create a 300-year timeline that all children could contribute to. Alternatively, children could create their own. Ask them to choose an aspect of the history of science to research, then add key dates and events on their timeline, e.g. famous science events, scientists and their inventions, the history of household appliances, or lighting in homes. Alternatively, children could research the symbolism of holly in Druid, Celtic, Roman and Christian traditions.

Alphabet garden

Science topic
Plants

Activity type
Identifying, classifying and grouping

Resources
Clipboard

Optional – camera

Pencils, paper

Plant identification keys or books

Tablet computer with plant identification app.

Overview
This activity is based on children searching for and identifying plants or other items in the school grounds and linking them to the alphabet.

ACTIVITY

- Children work outside with their clipboard, pens, paper and identification keys or books to find and identify different plants. Include 'weeds', trees and other plants.

- Look at the first letter of the plant's name and try to find one plant for each letter of the alphabet. As children work, they could also take photographs of each plant they find.
- You could invite a relative, or friend of the school, who has plant knowledge to support the children in identifying the different plants.
- Groups may decide to organise themselves so that they work in pairs to halve the workload.
- Once completed, gather the children together and ask them to look at their results. Which letters was it easiest to find a plant for? Which letters of the alphabet do not have any plants? (This is likely to include letters Q, X and Z.)
- Back in the classroom, either as a class research project or a home/school activity, challenge the children to find plants that begin with the missing alphabet letters. You might like to have a rule that they have to find plants that could be grown in the UK or their school gardens, e.g. Zinnias, which are daisy-like flowers.

The following is an alternative approach to an outdoors alphabet.

- On the school playground, children chalk a large, widely spaced alphabet A–Z. For example, give each child a piece of chalk, assign a letter of the alphabet to them and then ask them to spread out. Ask children to write their large letter where they are standing.
- Tell children to hunt the school grounds for items beginning with any letter of the alphabet. If they are collecting, for example, plant specimens, they are only allowed to offer one leaf.
- Children will need to identify their found items using identification resources.
- The children place their items next to the appropriate letter on the ground; alternatively, they could draw the item or list it using chalks if they are not able to move it.
- After about 15 or 20 minutes, stop the children and bring them together to look at which letters of the alphabet have the least/ most items. Then challenge them to focus on those letters that either have no items or the least items. Remind them that items can be natural or made.

- Once their list is completed, children could create individual, group or class alphabet books to display what they have found; the books could include photographs and sketches.

SCIENCE BACKGROUND

Plant scientists (botanists) classify plants into groups that have similar characteristics. The classification of plants results in an organised system for the identification and naming of plants. Carl Linnaeus was an important scientist who developed and refined a way to classify and name living things that is still in use today. Botanical sketches in science are important; some children could sketch specimens rather than photograph them. Show children illustrations from some of the great botanists from the past such as Charles Darwin, Beatrix Potter, Gregor Mendel, Carl Linnaeus, David Douglas and Robert Fortune.

CROSS-CURRICULAR LINKS

English

Since each child (or pair) will have a specific plant to sketch in the art activity that follows, they could research information about the plant, e.g. botanical name (Latin), life cycle, growing conditions, medicinal use, myths. Children then decide how to organise and present the information to create a fact file about their plant or use the information to annotate their sketch. Children could also research the lives and work of famous botanists and create a fact file that could be placed alongside a school 'Botanical Exhibition' or on the school website as an 'A–Z of Plants in our School Grounds' gallery.

If taking the alternative approach, ask children to choose an item from their letter, e.g. the child or pair with the letter A might choose 'apple core' from their list, or 'tarmac' for T. They then write a sentence or paragraph about the item, such as explaining what they think would happen to the apple core if left, or research tarmac and write some key facts about this material.

Art or Geography

Show children botanical sketches: these can be found on websites such as Google Images, Kew Gardens and The Natural History Museum. Discuss what they look like, how are they different from photographs and paintings? Give children the opportunity to explore sketching a plant from the 'Garden Alphabet' and then think about which parts of the sketch they are happy with and which parts they would like to improve. Their final sketches could be included in a 'Botanical Exhibition' or an online 'A–Z of Plants in our School Grounds' gallery.

This could be extended so that children work out the coordinates for the item that they found and place it on a large map of the school grounds. The result would be a large map with all the alphabet items on it, or the items listed next to the map with their coordinates for other children to work out where items were found. This could be used by other classes as an alphabet trail.

Caterpillar camouflage

Science topics
Living things and their habitats; Adaptation; Evolution and inheritance

Activity type
Pattern seeking

Resources
Collection pots

Different coloured string or wool 'caterpillars'

Sticky labels

Overview
Children collect 'wool' caterpillars of different colours to develop their understanding that some colours can be seen more easily in the environment than others, and that some animals use camouflage to avoid predators while others are brightly coloured as a warning to predators.

ACTIVITY

- Prior to the class going outside, make lots of different coloured 'caterpillars' by cutting up coloured wools. Scatter them outdoors over the top of grass or shrubs so they are visible. Include bright, dull and a range of colours found in the local environment.

- Group the children into teams and explain that they are going to search for 'caterpillars' around the grounds but only one person from each team is allowed to search for one caterpillar at any time.
- As a class, decide on the rules for this game, e.g. whether running is allowed, how teams will know when to start using the next collection pot, how the next team member will know when they are allowed to search, etc.
- Tell the children they will collect the caterpillars in pots labelled minute 1, minute 2, etc. so they know the order in which different colours were found.
- Give teams several minutes to find caterpillars according to the agreed rules.
- Once the time is up, give different groups one of the pots to sort and count how many caterpillars of each colour there are – for example, one group might have the 1-minute pot, another the 2-minute pot. They could record their data on a tally chart, or in a table on the school playground or on a wall surface.
- An alternative to putting the woollen caterpillars in a pot is to give each group a piece of card with several strips of Velcro® (hooked part) stuck on, labelled 'Minute 1', 'Minute 2' etc; the children stick each caterpillar to the appropriate piece of Velcro®.
- Children should share the data, looking for patterns, e.g. which colour caterpillars were found during the first minute, then the second, etc., and finally which colours were found during the final minute.
- Ask children to draw conclusions about colour and camouflage. What have they learned from this activity? Why do they think certain colours were found more quickly than others?
- Ask children to explain why some caterpillars use colour for camouflage and to find out if there are caterpillars that use other approaches to avoid predators.

SCIENCE BACKGROUND

Camouflage is an adaptation that allows some animals to blend in with certain aspects of their environment to increase the chance of survival by hiding them from predators. Camouflage is also used by some predators to help them hide so their prey does not see them coming. Some animals have evolved to use bright colours to warn predators not to eat them, because, for example, they are poisonous.

CROSS-CURRICULAR LINKS

Art
Children research and copy patterns on animals, e.g. butterflies, snakes, zebras, etc. Using a cut-out paper animal – e.g. a moth or butterfly – challenge children to design an effective camouflage for a specific habitat. Children can photograph the camouflaged animal against the habitat/background to be displayed around the classroom or in a class book. Use children's work to encourage them to think about which type of camouflage is most effective and why.

Mathematics
The data from the caterpillar collections can be transferred to a bar graph: 'A graph to show which colour caterpillars were collected at different intervals'. Challenge children to annotate the graph to explain why different colours were more easily seen than others. Introduce 'new colour caterpillars' and ask children to decide where on the graph the new colour caterpillars would go; in this way children use data to predict new values.

Run-around sound

Science topic
Sound, pitch and volume

Scientific enquiry
Classification

Resources
Chalk or skipping ropes for Carroll diagram

Card labels for rows and columns, e.g. high, low, loud, and quiet

Noise makers, e.g. musical instruments, boom whackers, noisy toys, sound effects by teacher's voice, mobile phone or tablet

Overview
In this activity children play a game that links sound and mathematics.

ACTIVITY

- With children, practise identifying high- and low-pitched sounds. This could include children using their voices to create quiet, loud, high and low sounds and also combinations, e.g. a low, quiet sound. Outside, prepare a giant 2 × 2 Carroll diagram using chalk lines or skipping ropes.

	Loud volume	Quiet volume
High pitch		
Low pitch		

- Label columns as high/low pitch and rows as loud/quiet volume as shown in the diagram.
- Ask children to run to any of the four boxes on the diagram and stop. Then sound a noise maker (e.g. cheeping chick – high and quiet; horror scream – high and loud; lorry engine – low and loud; cat purring – low and quiet). Shout 'Run-around sound' when the sound is heard, which is the signal for children to change position by moving safely to the correct box.
- Children could draw their own grids on the playground and repeat the activity, working in smaller groups.
- Discuss whether there are any patterns between the pitch of a sound and features of the object that produced it.

SCIENCE BACKGROUND

Volume and pitch are distinct properties of sound. Volume measures how loud a sound is and is related to the size (amplitude) of the vibration. A larger vibration makes a louder sound and a smaller vibration makes a quieter sound. Pitch measures how high or low a sound is and is related to the speed (frequency) of vibration. A high-pitched sound is made with a high frequency (fast vibrations) and one with a low frequency (slow vibrations) will make a low-pitched sound.

CROSS-CURRICULAR LINKS

Mathematics

Recap how to use a Carroll diagram for sorting objects or grouping things in a yes/no way. Label the columns as girls and not girls (boys). Ask children to sort themselves into girls/boys using the two boxes in the top row of the diagram. Then give another criterion to the lower row, e.g. age under 9 years/not under 9. Some children will need to move to the box below. Check children are in the correct box. Repeat using different ideas for criteria if necessary, ensuring they are yes/no choices. Hopefully the children will now be ready to play the Run-around sound game.

Music

If children have designed and made their own musical instruments (as part of a science topic on sound), they could be challenged to compose a piece of music for their instruments. The challenge is that children should use volume and pitch in their composition. Alternatively, children could provide the sound effects for a poem or story, using their voices or sound makers.

Birdsong

Science topics
Animals; Sound

Activity type
Identifying, classifying and grouping

Resources
Portable sound system, e.g. a tablet computer with birdsong recordings

Optional APP for birdsong recognition and identification

Overview
Children listen carefully to the birds in their school environment. They learn why birds make sounds and that birds can be identified by listening to birdsong.

ACTIVITY

- Take children to an area where they are likely to hear birds. Tell them to lie down or sit quietly and close their eyes, focusing on being quiet, concentrating and listening carefully to birdsong.
- Ask the following questions.

  - How many different sounds can you hear? Can you hear birds?
  - How many different kinds of birds can you hear? How do you know?
  - Do you know the names of some of the birds you can hear?

- Why do you think birds make sounds? (Compare to other animals, e.g. warning, mating.)
- Can you mimic (copy) some of the bird sounds that you have heard using your voice?

- Play children a selection of recorded birdsongs, e.g. wood pigeon, blackbird, blue tit. (Free recordings can be downloaded from BBC Radio 4; see Online resources at the end of this activity.) What do the children notice? How are the birdsongs the same? How are they different? Do they repeat a pattern of sound? How well can the children mimic the sounds?
- Ask children to classify the sounds in the environment, including birdsongs, as high/low, long/short and loud/quiet.
- Challenge children to choose a bird they can hear in the school environment and imitate it. Back in the classroom, children research information about a bird they have chosen, e.g. appearance, nesting, feeding, predator–prey relationships, their young.
- Repeat this set of activities across the seasons to develop children's ability to recognise different birds and find out whether the birds in the school environment are visitors or permanent across the different seasons.

SCIENCE BACKGROUND

Birds use their voices to communicate with other birds as a warning, to mark territory or when mating. This is an efficient way to communicate over distance. Like humans, birds create their song by vibrations: the bigger the vibration, the louder the sound; and the smaller the vibration, the quieter the sound. They can also change pitch; the faster the vibrations the higher the sound; the slower the vibrations, the lower the sound.

CROSS-CURRICULAR LINKS

English and Computing
Children produce observational sketches or download pictures of birds in the school grounds then research information, taking notes and representing the information as a fact sheet. These could be laminated and displayed around the school grounds as part of a wildlife trail. Children could also include a QR code which links the reader to additional online information about each bird.

Music
Play copycats where the children imitate a birdsong, first copying with voices then clapping the rhythm. Children listen to each other and try to identify the bird. Transfer the rhythm to percussion instruments, e.g. claves, guiros. Develop this further using chime bars to mimic the changes in pitch of the birdsong rhythm. Children could then compose a short, original birdsong for an imaginary bird using rhythm and pitch.

Online resources
www.bbc.co.uk/radio4/science/birdsong.shtml

ACTIVITY 13
Feed the birds

Science topics
Living things and their habitat; Seasonal change

Activity type
Comparative testing, identifying and classifying

Resources
Binoculars

Bird identification charts or books

Bird seed, e.g. Niger seed, mixed seed, sunflower (avoid peanuts due to pupils with food allergies)

Chalk

Recycled materials, e.g. plastic bottles, milk cartons, yoghurt pots

String and scissors

Overview
Making and hanging bird feeders is great fun; it offers the opportunity for children to develop their understanding of seasonal change and what different birds eat across the year. By observing and identifying birds, children learn about the differences and similarities among bird species, needs of living things and bird behaviour.

ACTIVITY

- Begin by engaging children in creating a bird 'I wonder …?' wall outside where they can chalk their questions about birds visiting the school grounds. Challenge children to use a wide range of question stems, for example, 'I wonder …

  - … which birds visit the school grounds?'
  - … what the birds eat; do all birds eat the same things?'
  - … why birds have different beaks?'
  - … if all birds eat the same food?'
  - … why we feed birds?'
  - … what we should feed the birds?'
  - … if we could make our own bird feeders?'
  - … where we should put our bird feeders?'
  - … why birds sing?'

- Children carry out a survey of birds visiting the school grounds using binoculars and identification charts or books to name the birds. A bird hide could be created for groups of children to sit in while carrying out the survey.
- Children could use a tally chart to record which birds they observed and which parts of the school grounds they visited, before making their bird feeders (and repeat this after the bird feeders are put in place to assess the impact of having the bird feeders).
- Children research what the visiting birds eat. For example, small seeds, such as millet, attract mostly house sparrows, dunnocks, finches and collared doves; robins and blue tits like mealworms; and, believe it or not, blackbirds like tinned dog food!
- The class could visit a supermarket or local pet shop to look at different kinds of bird feeders prior to designing and making their own using recyclable materials, e.g. milk cartons, yoghurt pots and plastic bottles.
- Groups could work on making various kinds of bird feeders including suet and seed balls using websites (see Online resources).

- Challenge children to think about where they will position their bird feeders, discuss predators, birds needing cover, and also how easy it will be to fill them, etc.
- Engage children in thinking about what other ways they could encourage different birds into the school grounds, such as creating microhabitats like wildflower areas or planting buddleia for birds to feed on.
- Join national events such as Birdwatch; as a whole class listen to recordings of BBC 4 *Tweet of the Day* to add another dimension to bird identification, as well as children learning to enjoy the sounds of nature in their environment.

SCIENCE BACKGROUND

Different types of birds have different dietary preferences. For example, they may eat other birds and animals, fruit, seeds, insects, molluscs, tree sap or a combination of these. Observing, identifying and then feeding birds throughout the year supports children in deepening their understanding of living things. Making detailed observations is central to supporting a range of learning, such as identifying and naming birds, life processes, habitats, life cycles and birds as part of food chains. Regular observations help children to develop good habits of thinking and working scientifically, modelling how scientists work.

CROSS-CURRICULAR LINKS

Mathematics
Children carry out surveys of birds visiting the school grounds before and after making their bird feeders. Ask children to create tally charts and then communicate their data using bar graphs of bird sightings in the school grounds, as well as types and amounts of food eaten daily by birds. Ask the children to use their graphs to conclude what effect the bird feeders have had on birds visiting the school grounds. Take part in national surveys and then use national

databases such as Birdwatch, which gives participating schools access to the final database and outcomes.

PSHE

This activity contributes to personal development by offering opportunities for children to ask and answer their own questions, developing their confidence and self-esteem in making their own decisions. Being able to work with others to make positive changes to their own school outdoor environment by feeding birds can contribute to helping children recognise that everyone has a responsibility to encourage and care for wildlife, and that their own decisions can influence the world around them.

Online resources

www.bbc.co.uk/programmes/b01s6xyk
(BBC Radio 4 *Tweet of the Day*)

www.bto.org/volunteer-surveys/bbs
(Birdwatch)

www.rspb.org.uk/discoverandenjoynature/families/children/makeanddo/activities/birdcake.aspx
(recipes for fat balls)

Popcorn feeders

Science topics
Living things and their habitat; Seasonal change

Activity type
Comparative testing, identifying and classifying

Resources
Bird identification picture resources

Darning needles

Large pine cones

Plain popcorn

Recording chart with pieces of popcorn or stackable cubes

Small bowls, e.g. shallow yoghurt pots

Thread

Overview
Children make different kinds of popcorn feeders to help feed the birds; they compare designs to find out which type(s) the birds like best. This activity could be repeated in different seasons to compare the results.

ACTIVITY

- Cook some plain popcorn kernels (avoid the sweet or salted variety) by following the instructions on the packet and allow to cool. You can make this in advance because popcorn that is two or three days old is less brittle than freshly made popcorn and is easier to work with. While this is an indoor activity, it is great for science if you make popcorn with children, teach change due to heat, reversible and irreversible change, and nutrition (plain popcorn as a snack is low in calories).
- Tell children that birds must hunt for their own food every day. During winter, birds especially need our help to find food. Ask the children what they know about the kinds of foods that birds like to eat, such as worms, seeds and fruit.
- Show the children a giant bowl of popcorn. Do birds like to eat popcorn? How can they find out? Give them time to discuss and reflect on their ideas and decide which ones they could try out.
- If the children have not come across threaded popcorn, show pictures, asking how this is made and why it might be a good way to feed birds.

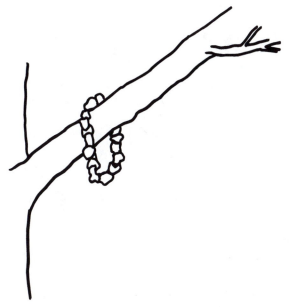

- This is a great activity to do outside, sitting on the ground and threading popcorn by carefully poking a large darning needle through a piece of popcorn and pulling the popcorn gently down to the bottom of the string, where a knot has been tied. When all of the string has been filled with popcorn, a knot needs to be tied to secure the other end. Some children may need help with this. The popcorn could then be hung up as a long string or the ends could be tied together to make a garland.
- Children could compare threaded popcorn with other approaches from their original ideas – for example, putting the popcorn into a small bowl, weighted by a stone so it cannot be blown away. If they think that decorating the bowl would make it more attractive to the birds, they could do this too.
- Some children may have some other ideas for feeders that you can use. One other idea is to use a pine cone and press the popcorn into the gaps between the scales of the pine cone.
- Ask the children where they think it would be best to place the feeders, e.g. in areas where they know birds will feed and where they can be observed without disturbing them, visible from the classroom window if possible.
- Explain that it may take the birds several days to find the feeders.
- Leave out identification charts, books and bird pictures for children to use to try to identify the birds they see.
- Each time they see a bird visiting one of the feeders they could record this in the classroom beside a photograph of the feeder by gluing a piece of popcorn onto a picture chart or by adding a cube to construct a tower of stackable cubes for each type of feeder over a period of time.
- Children could also record what kinds of birds are visiting the popcorn feeders.
- After a suitable time has passed, ask the children which popcorn feeder the birds liked best. Remind the children to look at the chart showing their results to help them decide.

SCIENCE BACKGROUND

Feeding birds throughout the year supports children in deepening their understanding of living things. Different kinds of birds feed in different ways. For example, some like to feed from the ground, such as robins; some like to hang upside down, such as blue tits. This means that different kinds of feeders (and foods) attract different kinds of birds to the school grounds. Elevated trays such as a simple bird table attract a wide variety of seed-eating birds such as pigeons, starlings and house sparrows. Mesh feeders, where the bird clings onto the mesh and pecks inside, are preferred by woodpeckers, nuthatches and jays. Hollow, finer mesh tubes with small perches underneath may attract smaller birds such as sparrows and finches. Regular observations help children to develop good habits of thinking and working scientifically.

CROSS-CURRICULAR LINKS

Physical education
Have a popcorn relay race! Small teams (three or four children) stand on one side of the playground. Each team has a large empty plastic bowl and a small plastic cup. On the opposite side of the playground, each team has a big container of popcorn to collect, one small cup at a time. Ready, steady, go! One member of the team runs across the playground, fills their cup with popcorn and brings it back across the yard. When they return to the rest of their team, they empty the popcorn into the empty bowl and pass the cup to the next team member who repeats the collection of popcorn in their small cup to bring back to their team's large bowl. The first team to fill the large bowl are the winners. This is definitely best played outdoors as the dropped popcorn can spread a long way. (Of course, the birds can eat what isn't swept up!)

Music
Make popcorn with children so that they can hear the sounds it makes while cooking. Ask children to find objects or instruments that they could use to copy the sounds. Children could listen to the song 'Popcorn' by Hot Butter and create a dance routine to the music outside, taking advantage of the freedom that the space offers. Children could explore the different sounds that can be made with hard un-popped kernels and with stale popcorn pieces,

using them to make percussion instruments, e.g. using different containers and shaking in different ways. How does the sound change if there is a mixture of kernels and popcorn? Children could record the sounds of their instruments using digital audio and compose for a performance with a popcorn percussion orchestra!

Online resources

www.naturedetectives.org.uk/packs/birds.htm

www.youtube.com/watch?v=KX_lnmb1Moo – 'Popcorn' (by Hot Butter)

Nest architects

Science topics
Living things and their habitat; Materials; Seasonal change

Activity type
Changes over time

Resources
Additional natural and recycled materials such as twigs, leaves, mud, straw, paper, fabric, plastic, string, rope, water (optional)

Bag to collect nest-building materials

Binoculars

Eggs to place in the nest (optional)

Tweezers to simulate bird beak (optional)

Overview
Children find out about different kinds of bird nests, then search for outdoor materials to build their own nest. They choose a place to site the nest and monitor it regularly, recording their observations over time.

ACTIVITY

- Sit in a quiet area outdoors and show the children how to use binoculars.

- Ask children to look at the environment around them. What can they see? (Examples may include houses, factories, trees, grass, ponds.)
- Spend some time sitting quietly, looking for animal life, especially birds. What are the birds doing? They could be nest building, finding food, defending their territory, etc.
- Ask the children to think of some reasons why birds build nests. They may have the common misconception that birds live in nests, but birds usually only build nests for holding their eggs and rearing chicks. Different birds build different kinds of nests. Not all birds build nests. (See Science background.)
- Discuss how birds use materials from the local environment to make their nests, e.g. natural materials (such as twigs, leaves, mud, straw) and made materials (such as paper, fabric, plastic, string, rope).
- Tell children to work in pairs and give them a bag to collect materials to make their nest. You may decide to provide additional natural and made materials such as those listed earlier and some water to make extra mud. Be prepared for muddy children!
- When they have plenty of materials, allow the pairs of children to construct their nests. You could put one or more restrictions in place, e.g.: a size to hold two eggs; using tweezers only to simulate building with a bird's beak; not being allowed to use human speech, only bird sounds.
- If the children ask for help, you may suggest mixing the mud with leaves or grass, or providing cushioning craft feathers or leaves in the middle of the nest to stop the eggs from breaking.
- When the nests are finished, allow half the class to visit some other children's nests to listen to descriptions and explanations of how those nests were constructed. The children listening offer constructive comments. After 10 minutes, swap over so the other half of the class can present their nest designs in the same way.
- Ask children to find a safe place for their nests so that they won't be damaged at playtimes. They may choose to put them in bushes, low branches of trees, behind benches, on top of a wall, etc.

- Children should record what their nest looks like in place. They could photograph it daily or weekly to record how it changes over time and suggest reasons for what might cause the changes.

SCIENCE BACKGROUND

Many species of birds build nests to lay and incubate their eggs in, and to raise their chicks in. Many birds build a new nest each year. The most familiar design to children is usually the cup nest, named after its shape. For some species, a nest is simply a shallow depression in the ground, a hole in a tree or building, a burrow in the ground, a woven structure or a mud dome with an entrance tunnel. Not all bird species build nests; some lay their eggs straight onto the ground or on rocky ledges, while others (such as the cuckoo) lay theirs in the nests of other birds. Nests are mainly used for breeding, although they may sometimes be used for roosting.

CROSS-CURRICULAR LINKS

English
Ask children to research one particular species of bird. For example, they could find out about what kind of nest it makes, how many eggs it typically lays, which habitat it prefers to live in, what its chicks look like and what the parent feeds the chicks. Children could present their research as either a fact card or a non-chronological report using appropriate features such as a title, an introductory paragraph and further paragraphs on different aspects of the subject, usually written in the present tense. It may also include sub-headings for each paragraph, illustrations with labels and/or captions, lists of facts in bullet points, technical vocabulary in bold and possibly a glossary at the end.

History
Ask the children where humans raise their young. Make it clear that bird nests are used for raising the young birds and then often abandoned, but humans continue to live in their home after their

children have grown up. Which materials do children think human homes were made of in ancient times and what they are made of now? Children research homes through history, looking at how people have made shelters from different natural and manufactured materials, e.g. wood, stone, air-dried mud bricks, fired clay bricks, glass, concrete, etc. They could then make a class timeline showing different shelters that they have researched and the materials they were made from.

Online resources
www.nationalstemcentre.org.uk Search eLibrary for Birds' Nests: Marvels of Architecture and Design.

ACTIVITY 16
It's dinnertime!

Science topic
Living things and their habitats – food chains

Activity type
Pattern seeking; Identifying, classifying and grouping

Resources
A4 card and pens (to make arrow cards)

Either card labels, cardboard headbands or small toys to represent living things within a food chain

String

Tall hat decorated with a picture of the Sun (optional)

Overview
Children use prior knowledge about feeding relationships and food chains to take the role of a plant or animal in an outdoor game relating to some of the living things in their school grounds. Food chains and predator–prey interactions are explored. Then children research food chains from other habitats to extend the game.

ACTIVITY

- Take the children outdoors and tell them to look around. Ask if they can see anything that is part of a food chain, e.g. birds, grass, snails, ants, trees, etc. Explain that every habitat will have its own food chains. Most habitats have lots of plants and fewer animals; ask for children's ideas about this.

- Explain that the children are going to carry out some activities taking the role of a living thing. This can be done in several ways. They could hold a labelled card, wear a labelled headband, or hold a small plastic or cuddly toy to represent their living thing.
- In the first instance, a simple food chain such as grass–snail–bird–cat can be used. Divide the children into four groups – grasses, snails, birds and cats – and label each using your chosen system of cards, headbands, etc. Ask the 'grasses' to stand still near you and explain that the animals are going to jog around until you shout, 'It's dinnertime!'. On this signal, they jog to find one thing they would like to eat, link up with that person and keep moving until all the animals have found one thing to eat and linked up in chains.
- Check that each child is correctly placed in the chain. The grass should link to the snail, which links to the bird, which in turn joins to the cat. (A child may point out that their cat eats grass. Make a mental note to come back to this later when discussing food webs.)
- If the children need more practice with getting into food chains, ask them to swap their living thing with another person and repeat, 'It's dinnertime!'.
- Ask the 'cats' where their food energy comes from in this food chain, where 'birds' get their food energy and where 'snails' get theirs. Finally ask the 'grasses'. Some may suggest the soil, so you might need to remind children that: 'Plants make their own food in their leaves using energy from the …' Children may be able to complete the sentence by saying 'Sun' and be aware of the process of photosynthesis.
- At this point, it is fun if you could put on a ridiculously tall hat decorated with a huge picture of the Sun to show how important you are!
- Tell the children that, in a food chain, arrows show the direction in which the energy travels: the grass provides energy to the snail. Ask a 'grass' child to hold an arrow card where the arrow points to the 'snail' child because the energy is flowing in that direction. Ask all of the food chains to use arrow cards to show the direction of energy transfer.

- Develop the use of vocabulary such as 'herbivore', 'carnivore', 'predator', 'prey', 'producer', 'consumer' using their food chains.
- Ask groups of children to carry out research into food chains from different habitats and make their own cards for the living things such as the examples below.

  - **Pond:** pond weed–tadpole–great crested newt–heron.
  - **Garden:** dead leaves–millipede–frog–hedgehog.
  - **Grassland:** dead grass–worm–shrew–owl.
  - **Hedge:** dead leaves–worm–song thrush.

- Outdoors, ask each group to play 'It's dinnertime!' again, using their own food chain with another group. The arrows should be added and peer assessment of the final food chain carried out. Groups could be swapped several times so that children can experience several food chains.
- Gather the class together to sit in their group food chains and ask each child to say which living thing they are. If they have the same animal or plant as someone else, use a piece of string to link these across the food chains. For example, the worm would link to both the shrew and the song thrush; the dead leaves would link to both the worms and the millipede. Use this to demonstrate how many living things are part of more than one food chain and eat more than one kind of food in order to meet their food and energy requirements. These interconnected food chains form a food web.
- Explore what would happen if the number of worms decreased or they even became extinct. How would this affect the other living things in the food web?

SCIENCE BACKGROUND

A food chain represents the transfer of food from a source to one or more living things (organisms), when one living thing eats another. The transfer of food is also a transfer of energy. Most food chains start from a green plant, which uses energy from the light of the Sun to make its own food through the process of photosynthesis. A food chain follows just one path as animals find food and the arrows in a food chain point in the direction of energy flow. A food web shows how several food chains are interconnected within an ecosystem.

CROSS-CURRICULAR LINKS

English

Children often find the vocabulary involved with food chains challenging. Ask them to make a mini picture dictionary for food chains with a page explaining each word, including a definition and illustration. They could start by listing which words they feel it is important to include – e.g. 'herbivore', 'carnivore', 'omnivore', 'predator', 'prey', 'decomposer', 'producer', 'consumer', etc. – and putting them into alphabetical order.

Music

Children use the topic of food chains to compose a short song. This could form part of a class composition with a repeated, shared chorus in unison and each group singing their own verse within this structure. It may be extended by some children who could sing their verse as a 'round' (like 'Frère Jacques' or 'London's Burning') where everyone sings the same song but each person starts one line later than the previous person so that different parts of the melody coincide in the different voices, but fit harmoniously together.

Observing change outdoors

Science topic
Seasonal change

Activity type
Observing over time and pattern seeking

Resources
Binoculars

Chalks

Hand lenses or Fresnel lenses

Map of the school grounds (on paper, tablet computer or chalked on the ground)

Optional – tablet computer, cameras, video

Overview
In this activity children explore, observe and record different changes in the school grounds.

ACTIVITY

- Take children outside and ask them to spread out, stand still and look around them, turning once slowly on the spot to observe the full 360-degree view.

- Ask children whether they think this place has always looked like this. How did it used to be different? Do they think it might change in the future?
- Tell children that this is an exciting place because change is happening right now, all around them.
- Ask children to discuss and predict what kind of changes they might be able to find evidence for. Record them on the playground surface or wall. You could provide a 'Word Wall' with key scientific vocabulary to prompt children's thinking and observations, e.g. change, different, cause, effect.
- Give children a map of the school grounds either in paper form, chalked on the school grounds or on a tablet computer. They could also photograph or video the changes that they observe.
- Children use the map to record, by annotating or using a key, where they have found evidence of change. For example, dandelions cracking tarmac, shadows changing shape or position over the day, birds making a nest, holes in leaves, cloud formations altering, wind making branches sway, puddles forming or disappearing, plants growing.
- Children could decide how to record the changes and their causes, e.g. using a two-column table or on a spider diagram with the central word 'Changes' drawn on the playground.
- Ask the class to return to base and, using chalk, write or draw the changes they have observed on the playground surface or a wall, including:

  - different kinds of change
  - what caused the changes
  - whether they were short or long term
  - whether they were reversible or irreversible.

- Ask children to think about and discuss with a partner what they have found out about change in the school grounds.
- Children use discussion in order to learn; they elaborate and explain clearly their understanding and ideas about change in the school grounds, using scientific technical terms such as: cause, effect, reversible, irreversible.

SCIENCE BACKGROUND

The world is a constantly changing place; some changes occur quickly and are easy to see but others are slow and difficult to detect without long-term repeated observations. Outdoors in the school grounds, the Sun evaporates moisture, can melt substances, rain dissolves some solids or changes materials in other ways, the wind can blow away sand, soil or damage structures, while freezing temperatures change the state of liquids to ice. Animals also have an effect on the environment, building homes, collecting materials, eating plants, while plants grow and create shade or crack tarmac. Many of these changes occur regularly in the school grounds and few people notice them; this activity focuses children's observations on changes taking place 'under their noses', and makes links between cause and effect.

CROSS-CURRICULAR LINKS

Geography
Children explore the school grounds, getting to know key features and how they change, using geographical skills to create and use resources such as maps and photographs. They demonstrate an understanding of how their environment changes over different periods of time and how humans can affect the school grounds by their actions, both positively and negatively.

Computing
Children decide how they would choose to change their outdoor area. If they were given an area that could be developed, this would give a real purpose for their work. Children use software to create a map of the current area including key features. Using this first map, they edit to move or delete some of the current features and add new ideas to redesign the outdoor area.

ACTIVITY 18
Natural weaving

Science topics
Materials; Seasonal change

Activity type
Identifying and classifying

Resources
Camera

Card weaving frame

Natural materials

Recyclable materials

Sticks

String

Wool

Overview
This activity focuses on weaving using natural materials to make the frame and for weaving. Alternatively, children could weave using fencing or plastic mesh fixed to a fence.

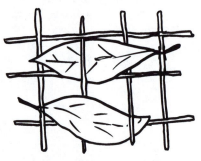

ACTIVITY

- Begin by showing children various weaving designs using natural materials. Depending on children's experience with weaving, you might have to teach or remind them how to weave.
- Younger or less experienced children could be provided with a standard card weaving frame ready-made for them, and weave in a range of natural materials.
- Alternatively, children could make their own frames using sticks or twigs from around the school grounds. There are different ways to make twig frames, e.g. tying four sticks together to make a frame, then tying string or wool from top to bottom to create the warp. Some children might prefer to make a Y shaped frame where the warp goes across the Y.
- Once their frame has been made, ask children to think about what they want to weave into their frame, focusing children on observation skills in choosing which natural objects they want to use, e.g.:

  - the same materials
  - shades of the same colour or different colours
  - whatever they can find walking in a straight line
  - natural materials that show seasonal colours, e.g. colours of autumn, reds, oranges, gold and browns.

- It might be best for children to start with small frames, so that they build up their expertise and confidence with natural weaving. Once they have had success with a small weaving project, they could move onto larger projects.
- Children could work with a partner to create a larger piece of natural weaving, which might be woven in such a way as to create a picture, e.g. grass, sky and twigs to form trees, or flowers woven in as part of the scene.

- Some children might mix natural and made (recyclable) materials to create different effects.
- Do encourage children to try natural weaving at home and bring their creations to school to share.
- Give children time to photograph their weaving or produce a short video clip explaining how to weave using natural materials. As part of this record, ask children to identify and classify the natural materials that they use, e.g. name leaves, grasses, flowers, the kind of twigs, etc.
- To complete this work, create a natural weaving exhibition outdoors for other classes and parents/guardians to visit.

SCIENCE BACKGROUND

Science in itself is a creative subject, demanding that children problem solve, linking together different ideas to create new knowledge, and taking risks by, in relation to their own experience, thinking the unthinkable. These are some of the hallmarks of creativity; in any area of understanding, linking art with science is a natural extension of creativity in science, bringing together skills in weaving with an understanding and appreciation of the beauty and delicateness of the natural world. This includes observing shades of colour, textures, form, and different kinds of grasses or flowers to create contrast. Children could also research animals that use weaving, e.g. orb weaving spiders and weaver birds.

CROSS-CURRICULAR LINKS

Art
In this activity children build their confidence and understanding in weaving by exploring both natural and made materials. Key aspects to focus on include the development of children's understanding of texture, colour and pattern alongside the planning, designing and making elements of weaving as children explore its vocabulary, e.g. weft, warp, weave, texture, colours and patterns. As part of the weaving process, encourage children to

articulate their ideas, choices and also evaluate the end product – whether they think it turned out as they wanted, what they liked best and if there was anything they would have changed or done differently.

Geography

Weaving is one of the oldest traditions in the world. In fact humans were weaving as long ago as the New Stone age – the Egyptians used weaving and the Chinese used silk, while people in India used the fibres of the cotton plant. Many different cultures have developed distinct patterns in their weaving and use natural materials for baskets, cloth, etc. Children could research weaving in different cultures, finding out about different techniques, the materials they used, and the patterns and colours used, e.g. Peru, Ecuador, Scotland, China and India.

Outdoor skeletons

Science topic
Animals, including humans

Activity type
Identifying, classifying and grouping

Resources
Access to natural materials such as twigs (for bones)

Digital cameras

Alternatively, small PE equipment for features such as joints, e.g. bean bags, skipping ropes, cones

Pictures or X-rays of a human skeleton, fish, bird, amphibian, reptile and a different non-human mammal

Overview
Children use natural materials or small PE equipment to model skeletons of animals with spines (vertebrates).

ACTIVITY

- Ask groups to collect resources – either natural materials from the school grounds or PE equipment – to make a model to show their prior knowledge of what they think a human skeleton looks like on the ground. Children could photograph their model.
- When complete, ask each group to share their ideas about their model skeleton's features. Encourage them to use scientific language.
- Then give children pictures or X-rays of a human skeleton to study and compare with the model they have made.

- Working in their groups, children discuss and agree what they would like to change on their original model skeleton and then make the changes. They photograph the second model.
- Again, each group spends 2 minutes explaining to another group what changes they have made and why this second model is more accurate than the first.
- This activity can be extended to other classes of vertebrates, e.g. fish, birds, amphibians, reptiles and non-human mammals. Challenge children to identify similarities and differences between the different classes of animals based on their skeletons.

SCIENCE BACKGROUND

Classification is the method used by scientists to put living organisms into groups with similar characteristics. Animals with a backbone (spine) are called vertebrates. The different classes of vertebrates are fish, birds, amphibians, reptiles and mammals. Comparing the structure of skeletons from different animals helps to extend and deepen children's understanding of the skeleton by applying their knowledge in different contexts.

CROSS-CURRICULAR LINKS

English and Computing
Groups look at their 'before' and 'after' photographs of the human skeleton. Then they work on a short oral presentation to explain how their ideas about the human skeleton changed or developed after improving their model. Children could use digital media to video the presentation, self-assess their work and act upon their self-evaluation to improve their presentation.

RE
Explore creation stories from different religions, e.g. Buddhism, Hinduism. In Christianity, the Genesis creation narrative tells how God created the world in seven days; fish and birds were created on one day and other animals on another day. If appropriate, introduce evolution as an alternative idea through exploring the life of Charles Darwin. Ensure that the school's policy for RE is followed.

ACTIVITY 20

Excavating bones

Science topic
Animals' skeletons

Activity type
Grouping, classifying and identifying

Resources
Metal spoons

Paintbrushes

Plastic containers

Sterilised bones from the butchers from 2 or 3 animals

Or laminated pictures of bones

String

 Safety: See *ASE Be Safe!* for guidance on using animal bones.

Overview
Children excavate bones that have been buried and use them to predict what the complete skeleton of an unknown animal may have looked like.

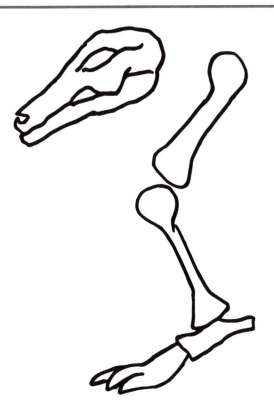

ACTIVITY

- Prior to the lesson, hide some sterilised or laminated bones in a safe area that could be excavated, e.g. soil or sand. Use string to divide the area into grid sections, place a bone or bones underneath the soil in every square and some objects on top so that children can practise naming squares using coordinates (e.g. A3).
- Show children some bones from the area where they were uncovered and explain that a palaeontologist found them and thinks there are more bones to find.
- Ask children if they know what a palaeontologist does.

- Ask what skills they think palaeontologists need to be good at their job – e.g. patience, curiosity, accuracy, organisation, teamwork – because they are going to work as a palaeontologist.
- Model how palaeontologists work, explaining they use a grid system to record where objects are found.
- Give pairs of children a square to excavate using a metal spoon, paintbrush and container in which to place the bone(s). Remind them to record where they found the bones using the grid coordinates.
- Once found, children observe their bone and discuss what is special about it. Ask children to suggest which part of the animal's body they think it came from and whether the bones are from one animal or several.
- Do the children think that all of the bones from the animal have been found? Why?
- The aim is for children to get together to see who has bones from a similar animal and share ideas about what kind of animal they think they have found (prediction).
- Of course, the children will not find a complete skeleton; usually palaeontologists do not either, so the next step is for the children to use the bones to think about what kind of animal they might have found. Ask them to imagine what it might have looked like and then chalk on the playground a diagram of the animal's skeleton with the bones they have found in place showing its location. Children could then label body parts that they think they have found.

SCIENCE BACKGROUND

Children should develop an understanding of how different scientists work. For example, palaeontologists study the history of animal and plant life through examining fossils (in this case real bones or laminates have been used rather than fossils). They use a range of skills from working scientifically including asking and answering questions, classifying and using evidence to draw conclusions alongside knowledge of rocks, animals and plants. Children could also research the work of palaeontologists such as Mary Anning and Dorothy Bate.

CROSS-CURRICULAR LINKS

Geography
Remind children of the conventions when using coordinates in geography – that you first move along the horizontal squares, then up the vertical squares to locate and name the square in the area for excavation. Draw a large grid with coordinates on the playground so that children record, using symbols, where they found their bones, resulting in a whole-class record that can be used for further discussion and questioning. This could be photographed and used as the focus of further work indoors at a later stage.

Art
Groups use their skeleton to draw what they think the creature may have looked like when alive. Talk about how illustrations of dinosaurs are predictions and no one really knows what they looked like, e.g. their colour, texture, etc. This may lead to a piece of artwork which could be a drawing, painting, collage or giant sculpture that could 'live' out in the area for a few weeks.

Dinosaur dimensions

Science topic
Evolution and inheritance

Activity type
Research

Resources
Chalk

Dinosaur information

Index cards

Laminated dinosaur name cards

Measuring equipment, e.g. tape measures, metre rules

Overview
This is a research activity which begins and ends outdoors. Children become experts on a type of dinosaur and present their research around a large-scale playground diagram of the dinosaur.

ACTIVITY

- Prior to the activity, hide laminated dinosaur name cards in the outdoor area. There should be one card to find per group (or several colour-coded letters that spell out a dinosaur's name).
- Ask groups of children to quickly find the dinosaur cards and return to base.

- Ask children how we know about dinosaurs, e.g. through fossils of bones, teeth, eggs, footprints, poo, etc., and remind them what fossils are.
- Ask each group to carry out research about their dinosaur indoors to make a 'fact file card' (e.g. index card) including, for example, a picture, whether it was a herbivore, carnivore or omnivore, and the size of the dinosaur, e.g.:

  - Diplodocus (up to 28m long)
  - Tyrannosaurus Rex (12–15m long)
  - Velociraptor (2m long)
  - Compsognathus (60cm long)

- Tell the children to take their fact file outdoors, and draw their dinosaur on the ground. This could be life-size or to scale (see Mathematics section). Children then use their fact file to label the important features of their dinosaur.
- Give the children some time to rehearse a short presentation about their dinosaur using the drawing and fact file, then each group presents their work to the rest of the class.
- The dinosaurs will be out on the school playground for the rest of the day and possibly the next if it does not rain, so children from other classes can access information about dinosaurs. Do encourage teachers and children from other classes to give feedback to your class.

SCIENCE BACKGROUND

English palaeontologist Richard Owen coined the term 'dinosaur' in 1842. Scientists use some basic rules to decide which ancient creatures are dinosaurs, such as they: lived between 250 and 65 million years ago; lived on land; had straight legs tucked underneath their bodies; and were reptiles. Within these basic rules, scientists group dinosaurs into different categories, e.g. using the shape of their hip.

CROSS-CURRICULAR LINKS

Mathematics

Groups of children draw a diagram of their dinosaur on the ground. This could be life-size or drawn to scale. Ask children how they will make sure it is the correct size and if necessary; suggest that they could first measure and mark it out with string, then draw around this with chalk. Label each dinosaur, and its height and length, with chalk. When finished, children measure other groups' dinosaurs to check they are accurate. If children have been working on scale in mathematics, they could 'scale up' or 'scale down' their dinosaurs and write the scale they used next to their dinosaur. Smaller dinosaurs could be scaled up and the largest dinosaurs, scaled down.

History

Children research how long ago dinosaurs lived. Dinosaurs lived in the Mesozoic Era which is divided into three periods: the Triassic, Jurassic and Cretaceous. Introduce mya (million years ago). This could be combined with the 'Toilet paper timeline', which is the next activity. Children could research and then create the background environment to their drawings of dinosaurs on the playground, e.g. drawing ferns and trees that were present at the same time as dinosaurs lived. If children are confident in using scale they could make sure the plants are the correct size in relation to the dinosaurs.

Online resources

www.nhm.ac.uk/nature-online/life/dinosaurs-other-extinct-creatures/dino-directory/about-dinosaurs/when-did-dinosaurs-live.html

Toilet paper timeline

Science topic
Evolution and inheritance

Activity type
Research

Resources
Cheap toilet roll(s) with approximately 500 sheets of paper

Felt tipped or gel pens which write on the thin paper

Index cards

Prepared labels from internet research

Sellotape® (for repairs if the roll tears)

Sticky labels

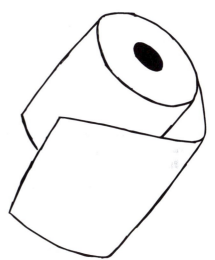

Overview
This activity helps to develop children's understanding of the large timescale of 'deep time' (from the formation of Earth onwards). The timeline of Earth is physically represented and key evolutionary points are highlighted in this activity using a toilet roll.

ACTIVITY

- In the classroom, children research evolution of life, from when Earth was formed to when humans appeared, creating a table of their results, e.g.:

  - 4,500 million years ago – Earth formed
  - 3,800 million years ago – first life (simple bacteria)
  - 530 million years ago – fish appear
  - 475 million years ago – land plants appear
  - 230 million years ago – dinosaurs appear
  - 200 million years ago – mammals appear
  - 160 million years ago – birds appear
  - 200,000 years ago – our own species, *Homo sapiens*

- Children create sticky labels for each of the key moments in the evolution of life: these will be placed on the timeline.
- Each group has one toilet roll (have some spare toilet rolls and Sellotape® to hand) which they take outdoors. Tell the children that each sheet of paper represents 10 million years.
- Label the start of the roll as 'Present day'. As they unroll it, children mark the boundaries of the squares (perforations) with a pen in 10 million-year increments until they get to 500 million years ago (50 sheets). Then, the label changes, so that they mark every tenth perforation in 100 million-year increments until they get to 4,500 million years ago.
- They should have used 450 sheets in total.
- Ask children to place the prepared sticky labels on the timeline, to show when different plants and animals appeared.
- When each group has completed their timeline, ask them to discuss their first impressions of the timeline and in particular, what they understand about when different animals (including humans) and plants appeared on Earth. Ask children to think about how this helped them to understand the history of Earth. Children could also research the evolution of human beings.
- Ask children to suggest how they could make a more permanent timeline in the school grounds. Have a class vote on suggestions and then create the most popular choice.

SCIENCE BACKGROUND

The main purpose of this activity is to show how small the amount of time that humans have inhabited Earth is in comparison to its history. This involves large numbers! One billion is now generally accepted as the American 1,000,000,000, so Earth is 4.5 billion years old. Evolution is the gradual changing of the features of living organisms through long periods of time to produce species which are in some way unlike the original ones.

CROSS-CURRICULAR LINKS

Mathematics
Each child writes the time that they represent on A4 card, e.g. Present day, 200 million years ago, and 400 million years ago. Children stand in line and shout out their time in order along the line (counting up and counting back). Twenty-three children would be needed to reproduce the whole timeline in the main activity, and any other children could wear labels with the key events and stand in the appropriate place on the timeline. Mix up the cards; children quickly reorder the timeline using their new card.

History
Create a timeline of historical events since humans first appeared on Earth, either global or related to British history, with each group researching an event and creating a 'fact file' card. Children could research topics such as civilisations, monarchs and inventions, scientific or geographical discoveries.

Fossil hunters

Science topics
Fossils; Living things; Materials

Activity type
Identifying, classifying and grouping

Resources
A collection of real or replica fossils (or laminated pictures) identified with a number label (one per group of children)

Chalk

Ruler to measure fossils

Overview
Children hunt for hidden fossils in the outdoor area. When found, they make a key to identify each fossil. It would be useful if the children have already experienced making identification keys prior to this activity.

ACTIVITY

- Hide the fossils in the outdoor area. Make a note of where they are so you don't lose them!
- Tell children that you have heard that the world famous palaeontologist Monsieur Coprolite has a problem. He was returning from an expedition and while flying over a particular area of the school grounds in his helicopter, his store boxes opened and some fossils fell out.

- Ask the children if they have heard the word 'coprolite' before (Monsieur Coprolite is a play on words; coprolite comes from the Greek – dung stone, and is, in fact, fossilised faeces or, as children will enjoy saying, 'fossilised poo'). Tell children that M. Coprolite would like them to help find the fossils and then create a large chalk identification key for the missing fossils on the school yard so that he can view it from the helicopter when he flies over.
- Tell each group of children to search for and find one hidden fossil. You may need to give a clue for any which aren't found quickly.
- Children look for observable features such as shape, size, pattern, etc. and turn these into yes/no questions.
- Discuss how some questions are better than others; e.g. 'Is it big?' is not as useful as 'Is it longer than 5cm?'; 'Does it have a pattern?' is not as useful as 'Does it have a spiral pattern?'
- You could have some yes/no questions prepared for the children to use if they find this tricky.
- Use the yes/no questions to make a whole class fossil identification key and chalk it onto the playground.
- When the identification key is complete, ask a child to walk each fossil along the lines to check that the key works, stopping at each question and taking the yes or no path in answer to the question and leading to the number of the fossil.
- Leave the identification key on the school playground and invite another class to use it, with your class taking the lead.

SCIENCE BACKGROUND

Palaeontology is the study of the history of life. Scientists who study palaeontology are called palaeontologists and they search for fossils to find out about the history of Earth. Fossils are plant and animal remains that have been preserved in or imprinted onto rock.

CROSS-CURRICULAR LINKS

English
Children write a letter to Monsieur Coprolite to tell him that the fossils have been found and explain about the identification key. Ensure that the conventions of writing a formal letter are followed. The class could later receive a response thanking the children for their observation skills and producing such a wonderful identification key.

Art/Design and technology
Children could design, make and evaluate a textile product such as a cushion cover inspired by their careful study of fossil characteristics. Set the context for the task: to make some new cushion covers for the reading area. There are many possibilities for applying a design to the fabric cushion cover, including fabric pens, collage and printable iron-on transfer paper (children would need to be supervised or an adult would need to iron the design onto the fabric).

Invertebrate microsafari hunt

Science topic
Living things and their habitats

Activity types
Identifying, classifying and grouping, and pattern seeking

Resources
Magnifiers

Children's fishing nets

Invertebrate identification cards or books

Plastic containers, e.g. yoghurt pots

Sieves

Soft paintbrushes

Trays, e.g. classroom trays, ice-cream 1l containers.

Two-way viewers

White sheets or plastic

Overview
In this activity children learn how to hunt for, collect and observe invertebrates in the school grounds.

ACTIVITY

- Remind children of their class rules for collecting and observing invertebrates or ask children to create their own, such as these:

    - Work quietly.
    - Respect invertebrates; they are living things.
    - Return them carefully to where they were found.
    - Only keep invertebrates for a short while and keep them in the shade.
    - Try not to disturb habitats too much.
    - If you can't identify something, make a drawing of it and look it up in books or on the internet.

- There are different ways to collect invertebrates; one is using a soft paintbrush and a plastic container, e.g. a yoghurt pot. When children find an invertebrate, they gently sweep it into the container using the paintbrush and then can either observe it in the container or gently move it to a larger container or a two-way viewer.

- Invertebrates live in microhabitats such logs, stones, leaf litter, soil and under leaves as well as on trees and shrubs. Children could, for example, lift up logs to find out what lives under them; others could carry out a tree or bush shake (where they shake branches and catch falling invertebrates on a white sheet or on white plastic); some children might dig up some soil or use a net to sweep grass and nettles to collect invertebrates.
- Leaf litter is also a microhabitat and children should find a range of invertebrates if they gently collect handfuls of dead leaves and twigs and put them in a soil sieve (or household sieves and colanders) with a large-sized mesh. Then they carefully sieve over a piece of white cloth or plastic and look for the animals that fall through. Children gently catch the invertebrates and place

them in a container or a two-way viewer to closely observe their features and how they move.

- At first, children will be so excited at finding different invertebrates that asking them to formally record anything can be counterproductive. Instead, visit different groups and encourage them to slow down, take their time and begin to observe the microhabitats and invertebrates in more detail, asking, for example, 'I wonder ...' questions, such as 'I wonder ...

  - ... where you found it?'
  - ... what the microhabitat is like?'
  - ... if you have any ideas why it lives there?'
  - ... if you know what it is?'
  - ... if it is an insect [six legs, three body parts and two pairs of visible wings]?'
  - ... if you have noticed anything unusual about it?'
  - ... if you know or can work out what it eats?'

- Provide cameras for children to use to photograph or video microhabitats. It is unlikely that cameras will be able to record small invertebrates, so focusing on microhabitats means that, when printed out, children can annotate them with names of invertebrates living there, conditions, food chains, etc.
- Do encourage children to use classification books, cards or sheets to identify and name the invertebrates that they find on their safari.
- Encourage children to get into groups to share what they have found out. Are there any patterns? For example, were most woodlice found in similar microhabitats? Where were spiders found? Were woodlice and spiders found in the same places?

SCIENCE BACKGROUND

The animal kingdom is divided into two main groups: vertebrates (animals that have a backbone such as mammals, birds, fish, amphibians and reptiles); and invertebrates (animals that do not have a backbone). The invertebrate group can then be divided into two groups. First are insects that usually have three pairs of legs, three parts to their body (the head, thorax and abdomen) and two pairs of wings (sometimes these are hidden under wing cases – e.g. ladybirds – or are very small). All other invertebrates are not insects, e.g. slugs, snails, millipedes, centipedes, spiders, worms. It is important for children to use the correct term 'invertebrates' rather than 'bugs' or 'mini-beasts', since this will help their understanding of the classification system.

Invertebrates live in small areas, e.g. under a stone; these are known as micro (small) habitats, so do introduce children to this word and use it regularly, encouraging them to describe what the microhabitats are like, e.g. cool, damp, dark.

CROSS-CURRICULAR LINKS

Mathematics
Children could re-visit microhabitats and carry out an invertebrate survey to find out where different invertebrates live and to carry out a population count. Using tally charts, children record how many of each invertebrate they observe in a microhabitat and then convert their tally chart into a bar graph or share their data with other groups. Children could enter their data into a spreadsheet to help them look for patterns.

Computing
The use of applications (apps) for identification of invertebrates can support children's learning. Apps should not replace the knowledgeable adult who can enthuse and inspire children to observe and remember invertebrate names and interesting information or the use of classification keys. The idea is that children use an app independently to identify the invertebrates that they find – for example, the OPAL Bugs Count app from the Natural History Museum. If children have access to more than one identification app, they could evaluate how effective each app is, devising their own criteria for success.

Comparing microhabitats

Science topics
Adaptation; Living things and their habitat

Activity type
Identifying, classifying and grouping

Resources
Camera (optional)

Clipboards, paper and pencils

Hand lenses

Plant and animal identification cards or books

Soft paintbrushes and plastic containers, e.g. yoghurt pots to collect small animals

Overview
Children choose two different microhabitats to investigate and compare. They describe the conditions of each microhabitat and find out how the conditions affect the plants and animals that live there. This activity is also useful if it follows the 'Invertebrate microsafari hunt' activity, during which children develop skills collecting and observing invertebrates.

ACTIVITY

- Remind children what a habitat is: a natural environment providing a home to living things, e.g. plants, animals, fungi, etc.

The habitat provides the basic conditions that the living things need to survive.

- Ask children to suggest what plants and animals might need to stay alive and keep healthy, e.g. water, air, warmth, food, home (shelter), light for plants, etc.
- Ask the children if they can identify more than one habitat in the school grounds and establish the idea of a microhabitat (small areas, e.g. under stones, under a log, among the grass, in leaf litter, in a bush, next to a drain, next to a pond, in the wild area).
- Ask pairs or small groups of children to choose two different microhabitats to explore and compare. Ask them to predict which living things they think they might find there.
- Remind the children how to take care of living things when searching for and identifying them, e.g. for plants and fungi; be careful not to break parts off. Remind children of their class rules for collecting and observing invertebrates (see the 'Invertebrate microsafari hunt' activity). Also remind the children how to correctly use a hand lens.
- Ask children to think of at least four adjectives to describe the microhabitat (e.g. dark, light, dry and damp, rocky, muddy, warm and cool) and record all of the living things they see on their clipboards. If possible, they could also take a photograph.
- Ask the children to spend 10–15 minutes exploring and recording each microhabitat.
- When they have finished, ask the groups to discuss which microhabitat had the biggest variety of living things, and why. Were there any similarities between the two microhabitats? Were there any differences?
- Ask children to use their clipboards to write about each microhabitat individually, then to write at least one sentence to compare them.
- Challenge children to explain how living things depend on each other, e.g. plants that provide a source of food and shelter for animals. Ask the children for their ideas about how the animals are adapted to the habitat in which they live.
- This activity could be repeated several times during the year, returning to the same microhabitats and comparing them across the seasons.

SCIENCE BACKGROUND

A microhabitat is a small habitat where living things exist. The living things in one microhabitat are suited to live in the conditions that exist there – e.g. moisture, temperature, light levels, food supply – and may not be able to survive as easily in another microhabitat. This is because all living things evolve, i.e. those with the most suitable characteristics for their habitat survive best and reproduce with these adaptations, until eventually the species evolves to become suited to its habitat. If the conditions in a habitat change, the living things there are affected and may not even be able to survive there any more.

CROSS-CURRICULAR LINKS

English
Discuss the effects of changing an environment to the animals living in that habitat, e.g. draining a pond, cutting down a tree or removing a hedge. Children could write a story about an animal trying to survive in a changing habitat or create a poster persuading people to protect and conserve the environment. Alternatively, give children a scenario, in the form of a letter or perhaps a 'mock up' newspaper headline which says that a local habitat (maybe part of their school grounds) is under threat from construction (e.g. a car park). Challenge children to think through the consequences for the habitat(s) and prepare reasoned arguments against the proposals.

Geography
Why are habitats around the world different? Ask the children to use maps, atlases and online resources to research physical geography – look for patterns in temperature, rainfall, etc. related to type of vegetation and habitat. Then think about human geography – how have humans changed habitats? This could lead to research into the impact of deforestation or the use of pesticides in farming.

Invertebrate adaptations

Snails

Science topics
Adaptation; Living things and their habitat

Activity type
Identifying, classifying and grouping

Resources
Camera (optional)

Clipboards, paper and pencils

Hand lenses

Plant and animal identification cards or books

Sketchbook or pad

Soft paintbrushes and plastic containers, e.g. yoghurt pots to collect small animals

Overview
Children collect and study snails, observing them and their habitats, sketching and making notes leading to asking and answering their own questions about snails. This activity can also be replicated using other invertebrates, e.g. slugs, worms and woodlice.

ACTIVITY

- Remind children what a habitat is: a natural environment providing a home to living things. Remind them also that, when they look for and collect snails, they should remember their own rules for working in the environment (see 'Invertebrate microsafari hunt').
- Before beginning this activity, check that you do have snails in your school grounds and that you know where they can be found; if there are none then you might want children to hunt for and collect invertebrates that are common, e.g. worms and woodlice.

- A useful piece of kit for children to make is their own question stem fan (like key word fans) prior to going out on their invertebrate hunt. Each section has a question stem written on it, e.g.:

  how   what   where   when   who   which

  what if   why   can   could   will

  Children can then use the question stems to ask a range of questions during this activity when they have observed and drawn their snail.
- Children set off on their snail hunt. When they find one or more snails they should record the habitat, by sketching, taking photographs or video clips and describing the conditions and

the plants, e.g. shady, under nettle or cow parsley leaves. Equipping children with plant guides is important so that they can identify and name plants where they find snails.

- Snails can be collected and observed in the field, placing them in a container with some of their food, and using a Fresnel lens or two-way magnifier so that children can see both the top and underside of the snail.
- Children love using a sketchbook or pad, so if they have one they could sketch their snail. Encourage them to draw their snail larger than life. Most children observe gross detail first, such as the shape, spirals and antennae. Encourage children to look again, and again, each time adding another layer of detail. Children should also annotate their sketches; even if they don't know scientific names for parts, they should give them a name and then research the correct term back in class.
- While they are still outdoors and observing their snail, explain to children that they are going to use their question stem fans to ask different questions about their snail. Encourage them to focus on questions that they cannot answer by observing the snail and its habitat, and tell them that they can only use each question stem once.
- When they have completed their observations and written their questions, they can decide, back in the classroom, how best to answer their questions, e.g.:

  - Will they have to do something, e.g. a comparative or fair test?
  - Do they need to carry out a survey?
  - Is the only way to find an answer to research using a book, video or the internet?

SCIENCE BACKGROUND

Snails are gastropods, and have many adaptations. They have one foot and a coiled shell that they can withdraw into completely. They leave a slimy trail by secreting a mucus which helps them to survive because it attracts water and enables the snail to stay damp as well as helping it to move.

Other adaptations include having eyes on stalks which can move inside out when the snail withdraws and extends them; this is the snail's way of protecting its eyes. In freezing or very hot temperatures snails secrete a mucus and seal themselves into their shells to protect them from extremes of weather.

For gardeners, the worst adaptation is that the snails are hermaphrodites – i.e. they have both male and female reproductive organs. Snail bodies have adapted for reproduction; they can change sex if necessary to procreate. In addition to their ability to change sex, some snails can self-fertilise and reproduce asexually. Snails will mate with each other, and fertilise the eggs in the other, so both of them will lay as many as 100 eggs each – one of the reasons there are so many snails in some gardens!

CROSS-CURRICULAR LINKS

English
Children ask questions to clarify and extend their understanding using question stems. The question stem fans challenge children to use a variety of different question stems, increasing the range which can lead to different kinds of ways in which children answer those questions, as well as different areas of knowledge.

Art
Use Google Images to show children the work of the artist David Klein, who created colourful and engaging illustrations of a range of animals – including a snail. These bright, multi-coloured pictures are easy for children to identify with and to emulate.

Children could also focus on the spiral patterns on snail shells, recreating them with string, paint, different wool and also as repeat patterns on large sheets of paper. Alternatively, give children dough to create snail models and paint them either in natural colours which replicate the colours of snails that they have found or in the colours similar to those used by David Klein.

Plant frames
Quadrats

Science topics
Biodiversity; Living things and their habitat

Activity type
Pattern seeking, identifying, classifying and grouping

Resources
Camera (optional)

Card circles and pens

Clipboards, paper and pencils

Hand lenses

Plant identification card

Quadrats of a standard size, e.g. home-made square frame quadrats or PE hoops

Overview
Groups of children use a frame 'quadrat' or PE hoop as a sampling tool to isolate an area of ground to survey in detail. They ask and answer questions about the biodiversity of sample areas in the school grounds by observing and surveying the plants inside the quadrat.

ACTIVITY

- Home-made frame quadrats can be made by tying four equal lengths of bamboo canes or straight sticks into a square with sides 1m or 50cm. Older children may be able to make the quadrat themselves.
- Check the area where the class will be working for hazards and make a preliminary survey to identify the most common plants. Collect one of each plant, attach it to a large piece of card and ask the children if they can identify (name) the plant. The board can then be displayed as a plant identification resource.
- Choose a random area on the school playing field. Place the quadrat (or PE hoop) flat on it. Ask the children which living things are inside the quadrat. They may not realise that there is more than just grass inside the quadrat and be surprised by the biodiversity in an area they think of as 'just grass'.
- Ask the children if they think that the long grass around the edge of the playing field has the same plants as the shorter grass in the middle.
- Encourage the children to think of some other questions to investigate, e.g. is the sunny side of a hedge home to the same living things as the dark area under the trees; are there more daisies in mown or uncut grass; which area has most dandelions; where are we most likely to find flowering grasses?
- Ask children to write their questions on card 'petals' (circles of card) and arrange them on the playground in the shape of a large flower, or create a chalk flower with petals.
- Ask each group to take one card 'petal' from the flower and discuss in their group how they could find out the answer to the question on the 'petal'.
- Prompt the group to consider how they will record their results. They may draw, count, devise a table or choose another way.
- Give the children time to carry out their investigations using the quadrats.
- When they have finished, ask each group to report back. Have they answered their question and come to a conclusion?
- Ask the children to write the answer to their question on the reverse of the card 'petal'. The large flower made of the card petals could be used for a classroom display.

SCIENCE BACKGROUND

Biodiversity describes the variety of different types of life found on Earth and it is a measure of the variety of living things present in different ecosystems. In this activity, the quadrat provides a standard size sample area to study, so that comparisons can be made between different microhabitats and meaningful conclusions drawn using patterns in the data collected. Simple frame quadrats are adequate for this enquiry; for more detailed surveys, though, grid quadrats that are subdivided into a grid of smaller squares may be used, with the quadrat positioned according to a random placement sampling method.

CROSS-CURRICULAR LINKS

Mathematics
If the children have chosen to count each type of plant to obtain their results, a frequency table and bar chart could be constructed to show what they found out. Some groups may have chosen to estimate a fraction or a percentage for each type of plant in their quadrat.

Art
Dandelion flower heads mature into spherical seed heads commonly called dandelion clocks. Research the 'A Thousand Wishes' artworks created by Denis Brown (Irish calligrapher). The wishes are engraved upon layers of glass to create a dandelion seed head-like design composed of layer upon layer of text so that the wishes remain mostly illegible and secret. Children could explore writing and drawing on translucent or transparent materials, e.g. tracing paper or clear plastics, and then layering the materials so that their secret wishes and designs are hidden within the artwork.

Lie down and listen

Science topic
Humans' senses

Activity type
Identifying, classifying and grouping

Resources
Chalk

Puppet or soft toy

Overview
This is a great calming activity to do outside, developing the children's ability to remain quiet and concentrate on sounds in their environment.

ACTIVITY

- Begin by introducing a puppet or soft toy as a new member of the class. The problem is the puppet is noisy, hyperactive and does not know how to listen well!
- Ask the children to tell the puppet about how we hear. Children should be able to identify the ears as the part of the body associated with the sense of hearing.
- Ask the children to think of advice to give to the puppet about good listening skills. What should it do?
- Suggest that the class goes outdoors to show the puppet how to listen and practise listening to sounds.

- Partner children in this activity and ask: 'I wonder what we will hear. What do you think?' Share predictions.
- Once outdoors, children lie down in a circle with their heads near to centre and their feet pointing to its outside. (This minimises eye contact with other children.)
- Use children's ideas shared with the puppet about good listening; ask children to breathe slowly and experience a minute or two of quiet relaxation. They might have suggested that the puppet should close its eyes so it can concentrate better. Ask them all to do this.
- If the puppet talks or interrupts, ask children to softly say 'Sssh' until everyone is silent.
- Ask children to raise a finger each time they hear a new sound and concentrate on remembering each one. You will know when it is time to bring this to an end as children become fidgety.
- Ask children to show the puppet how they get into groups. Give them chalk to draw and write on the playground to record the sounds they have heard.
- Allow time for the groups to look at what each one has recorded and spend a few minutes discussing which sounds the children heard most. Ask the puppet/soft toy what it learned today about listening.

SCIENCE BACKGROUND

We often hear sounds but do not notice them. Hearing refers to the sounds that you hear, whereas listening requires more than that; it requires focus. By lying down, relaxing and closing their eyes to remove the sense of sight, children can concentrate on using their sense of hearing to listen.

CROSS-CURRICULAR LINKS

English
While outdoors, spend some time engaging children in listening activities that discriminate between different phonemes in words.

They could name items that begin or end with the same sound, or play 'I can hear something beginning with ...'. Groups of children could work together to draw objects that they can hear outdoors with a given phoneme.

PSHE

Body language associated with listening in social interactions is important. In pairs, one child tells the other why they like a favourite place in the playground, e.g. there are trees which sometimes swish in the breeze. The listener should look away from the talker and give no eye contact. Repeat this with the body language of a good listener, e.g. eye contact, looking interested, not interrupting. Swap roles and repeat. Discuss how it feels to be the person talking and listening in each scenario and why it is important when someone is talking to pay attention to them.

Shadow faces

Science topic
Light

Activity type
Exploration

Resources
Access to natural materials, e.g. stones, leaves, twigs and feathers

Chalk

Overview
In this activity children explore making shadows on a sunny day and use natural materials to give human shadows faces.

ACTIVITY

- Before starting this activity, ask children to explain to each other how they think shadows are made, and how their own shadows are created.
- Children work with a partner and explore making interesting shadows including joining together to make shapes using both bodies.
- Ask children to choose their most interesting and creative shadow to share with another pair. As they show their shadow, they explain how the shadow is made, using correct scientific vocabulary, e.g.: light, straight lines, opaque, block.
- In the next activity, children collect a range of natural materials, e.g. stones, leaves, twigs and feathers. While one person stands

very still to make the shadow, the other (in discussion with their partner) draws around the shadow with chalk and then decorates it; for example, they could make facial features (eyes, nose, ears, mouth, eyebrows, eyelashes, glasses, beard, hair), use stones for buttons or a daisy chain for a bangle.

• When children are satisfied that their shadow is complete, they take a photograph of it, swap places with their partner and repeat the activity using the other person's shadow.

SCIENCE BACKGROUND

A shadow is made when an opaque object blocks light. The light cannot pass through the object and therefore the area behind the object is dark, hence the shadow. A transparent object will not make a shadow, because light can pass through it, so there is no dark area shadow. A translucent object can make a faint shadow. Key language that children should be encouraged to use when explaining how shadows are made includes: light, translucent, opaque, blocked, straight lines, light rays, dark.

CROSS-CURRICULAR LINKS

English
Children create a story where their own or another shadow comes to life and has an adventure. Children use different ways of constructing sentences and think about the effect on the character, setting and plot in order to develop suspense and surprise in their writing.

Physical education
Children could create shadow dances outdoors and share their performances with other children, who could offer considered comments to help improve the dance. Can they suggest how the dancers might throw some shapes in their dance which would create interesting shadows? Photographs could be taken to record and 'freeze frame' the body shapes with their associated shadows.

Playground constellations

Science topic
Earth and space

Activity type
Research

Resources
Chalk

Index cards

Reference material on constellations

Overview
In this activity children choose a constellation to research. They find out facts and the story behind its name, then they recreate it as a large constellation drawn on the playground.

ACTIVITY

- Working in pairs, children choose a constellation to research and make a fact file about it using, for example, index cards.
- Once their fact file is complete, children go outside onto the school playground, find a space, and use chalk to draw a large copy of their constellation, annotating it with its name and a sentence to explain the myth behind it. They could use a stone or pebble to represent each star in the constellation.
- When children have finished their outdoor constellation, they can wander round and learn about other constellations. If the

class is divided into two, then one half can visit the other and pairs share additional information using their fact file cards, then swap over.

- Since the constellations are drawn on the school playground it means that the rest of the school has access to them, and children will enjoy staying with their constellations either during playtime, or a specific time during the day when other classes can visit.

Invite parents to view the constellations towards the end of the day and listen to children talking about each one. This is a great activity if carried out during, for example, National Astronomy Week, and could be part of an evening astronomy activity for families.

SCIENCE BACKGROUND

A star is a massive ball of very hot gas which is held together by gravity. A constellation is a group of stars that often form a shape or pattern that helps us to recognise it from Earth. If you think of it like a huge dot-to-dot, where you join the dots to create a picture, then you have the pattern of a constellation. Over thousands of years humans have made up stories and legends about constellations to try to explain why they are in the sky.

CROSS-CURRICULAR LINKS

English
Children read and discuss information about constellations in reference books or online to create a fact file. This demands that children read with comprehension and extract specific and relevant information, recording it in concise note form. Children will also read about the myths and legends linked to constellations from different cultures and traditions, which they could share to different audiences, e.g. peers, parents, guardians. Children could lead a story-telling session where they retell a myth/legend to a younger or older audience sitting around one of the playground

constellations. Alternatively, children could enact as a play the myth behind their constellation.

Mathematics

The universe is huge and the numbers are equally big, so this type of science activity brings children into contact with large numbers and helps to develop a sense of awe and amazement of the sheer number of stars in the universe. For example, astronomers calculate that there are more than 100 billion stars in our galaxy and more than 100 billion galaxies in the universe. Ask children to find out how many millions there are in a billion and trillion. What would these numbers look like written down? What is a septillion, octillion, nonillion, googol, centillion and googolplex (the world's largest number with a name)?

ACTIVITY 31

Windy places

Science topic
Weather

Activity type
Comparative testing

Resources
Paper

Plastic bags

String

Tissue paper

Overview
In this activity children explore windy places around the school and design, make and test a wind sock to measure how windy it is in the school grounds.

ACTIVITY

- Prior to going outside, you could show children video clips of windy days from gentle breezes to storm-force winds. Also show children video clips or photographs of wind socks (e.g. at an airport) and ask them about why they are used.
- Obviously the best type of day for this activity is a windy one. Go outside and challenge children to say how they know that it is a windy day. What can they see, hear and feel?

- What do they think wind is? This is a challenging question for many children who might talk about what wind does, rather than it being moving air.
- Move to different places in the school grounds to find if some are windier than others or perhaps more sheltered. Give children a map of the school ground and ask them what kind of symbols they could use to put on it to show how windy it is in each place. Alternatively, children could create a simple scale, e.g. 1–4; 1 being no wind, and 4 being a gale.
- Remind children about wind socks and ask how they could be used around the playground so that everyone can tell which places are very windy and which are sheltered. Ask children to think about why this might be useful to know about, e.g. when it is very windy and cold and children want to take shelter.
- Back in the classroom, show children a range of pictures of wind socks so they can design, make and then test their own wind sock. Children could work individually or in pairs.
- As children are making their wind socks, encourage them to test them outdoors and make changes, e.g. by adding string or streamers.
- Once made, the children's wind socks can be placed in the school grounds so that the children can use them for weather observations related to the force of the wind.
- Ask children to think about how wind makes them feel, e.g. light breeze in summer, windy day in autumn, gale forces winds and rain. Encourage them to explain the reasons why they have different kinds of feelings for different kinds of windy days.

SCIENCE BACKGROUND

Wind is moving air and is an important element of weather; it is measured using the Beaufort Scale. Linking moving air to moving things that the children know can be useful; for example, wind can move as fast as a racing car – over 100 miles an hour. It is useful to mark the points of a compass on the school grounds so that the children know where east, west, north and south are. This is useful to help them work out the direction from which the wind is blowing; it is linked to the kind of weather we get. Winds from the north and east bring cold air from polar regions; winds from the west often bring rain; while winds from the south often begin in the tropics and are more frequent in the summer, bringing warm air as well as thunderstorms. Weather forecasters need to be able to measure and know the wind's direction so that they can forecast weather and warn people if winds are going to be strong and possibly damage buildings and trees.

CROSS-CURRICULAR LINKS

English
Children take on the role of presenter after watching weather reports on TV and YouTube. Ask children to think about what the weather presenter wears, what kind of map is used and the symbols on the map. What does the presenter say at the beginning, going round the UK, and then how does the presenter say goodbye to the audience? Children script and then video their presentation, reviewing it to critique their performance as well as that of other children in the class.

Mathematics
Children keep a weather chart on a daily basis and, using the data in their chart, are able to answer questions such as these.

- How many days were sunny, rainy, cloudy and cold?
- Which were the hottest and coldest days?
- Which was the cloudiest day?
- What were the coolest and hottest temperatures?
- Which day was the best day for playing outside?

Online resources
https://achildrenspoemaday.wordpress.com/category/childrens-poem/weather/
(weather poems)

www.canteach.ca/elementary/songspoems17.html
(weather poems)

Water cycle

Science topic
Materials – solids, liquids and gases

Activity type
Identifying, classifying and grouping

Resources
Chalk

Coloured objects to represent solid, liquid and gas so that children can have one of each

Large beach ball to represent the Sun

Poster of the water cycle

Overview
Children study a poster of the water cycle and use their understanding to model the processes involved in the school grounds on a large scale. In particular, they identify which state of matter they are modelling at any time using movement and a colour-coded object.

ACTIVITY

- Take a poster of the water cycle outdoors and attach it to a fence or wall so the children can study it carefully. Talk about how the water on Earth is part of a natural recycling system and show them how the poster represents this.

- Tell children they are going to act out and model the water cycle in the playground. Use chalk to draw three large areas: an ocean area, a sky area, and a land area with one or two rivers to flow back towards the ocean area. Use the beach ball to represent the Sun.
- Revise the states of matter – solid, liquid and gas – and name water in these states – ice, water and water vapour. Link each of these to a coloured object such as a ball, e.g.: a blue ball with 'S' written on it, a green ball with 'L' written on it and a yellow ball with 'G' written on it. You may wish to introduce the idea that water is made of water molecules (H_2O) but this is not essential.
- Each child will need all of these three coloured objects later on, and the colours will help you to assess their choice of ice, water or water vapour.
- Demonstrate how to be ice (stand still, shiver, and hold up the S object), how to be water (stand near to other people walking slowly and holding up the L object) and how to be water vapour (jogging around, spreading into spaces, avoiding other people and holding up the G object).
- Ask selected children to call 'water', 'water vapour' and 'ice' several times in a random order so that the class can rehearse the movements, holding up the correct S, L or G object each time.
- Now the modelling can begin. At the start, everyone is liquid water in the ocean, milling about holding up the L object to show that they are a liquid. The children will walk gently and smoothly around and past each other but must stay in the 'ocean'. The Sun provides energy so that some evaporation can occur at the surface of the ocean – call out the names of some children that you want to 'evaporate' and they can jog out of the ocean, holding up the 'G' object, towards the area that represents the sky. Ask most of the children to evaporate but leave some of them behind so that the ocean doesn't become empty.
- In the sky, ask about half of the children to become a liquid (condense), holding up the 'L' object, walking slowly as before, to become clouds.
- Discuss what clouds are made of. (Tiny droplets of water which can be seen, ice crystals and also invisible water vapour.) As some of these children come together, they can fall as rain by

walking to the land area, ask these to travel down the river back to the ocean area.

- Repeat this process, but make sure that the children who have been in the ocean all of the time are chosen to evaporate this time and those who have just travelled down the river remain in the ocean for a while.
- Repeat the cycle two or three times so that the children understand how the model relates to the poster and the water cycle itself.
- Ask the children where ice might form in the water cycle (e.g. in the sky area and moving towards the land area or even on the land if it is a cold day).
- Following this whole-class demonstration, divide the class into four groups and ask them to repeat in their groups the modelling of the water cycle.

SCIENCE BACKGROUND

Earth is covered with water, which is essential for life. The water cycle acts as a natural recycling system and it is driven by the heat energy from the Sun. Water evaporates from lakes, oceans, etc. and is transpired from plants. The water vapour rises into the atmosphere where cooler temperatures cause it to condense into clouds. Precipitation may fall as rain, snow or hail. Some groundwater runs off and flows into rivers; much of it soaks into the ground and replenishes aquifers, which store freshwater. Some groundwater finds openings in the land surface and comes out as freshwater springs. Over time, the water returns to the ocean ready for the cycle to start again. Humans intervene in the natural water cycle to provide the public water supply.

CROSS-CURRICULAR LINKS

Geography
Children research what happens when places have too much water (flooding) or not enough (drought). How does this affect what the

place is like? How does it affect living things there? This research could include a case study of one particular place so the children have time to carry out a detailed piece of work.

Art
Children study how water has been represented by various artists, e.g. Monet, Hokusai, Turner, Hockney, Escher, etc. They collect ideas in sketchbooks and choose some of these to develop in their own work in a range of media.

Message magnets

Science topic
Forces – magnets

Activity type
Fair and comparative testing, changes over time

Resources
A selection of commercially available fridge magnets as stimulus

Classroom magnets to test surfaces outdoors

Overview
Children predict where a small magnetic sign, like a fridge magnet, can be located in the outdoor area, e.g. on the exterior of the school building or within the school grounds. They test their ideas outdoors then design and make a 'Message Magnet'. After installing the 'Message Magnet' outdoors, they monitor how well it performs over time.

ACTIVITY

- Take the children outdoors and explain that later they will be making a 'Message Magnet' for the outdoor area in the style of a fridge magnet. Discuss the class theme for these, e.g. animal or plant facts, weather sayings or even a QR code.
- You may wish to show the children a selection of commercially available fridge magnets just in case they have not seen one before. (These generally comprise a picture or message attached to a small magnet so it can stick to a fridge door.)

- Ask the children to work in pairs to predict which places they think a magnet would 'stick' to and explain why they think this. Some children may say it has to be metal. At this stage, accept all ideas even though not all metals are magnetic. (See the Science background section.)
- Encourage the children to use scientific language, e.g. 'attracts' instead of 'sticks', and prompt them to consider the exterior of the school building as well as the school grounds. There may be fences, hedges, walls, sports facilities, drains, doors, trees, walls, waste bins, etc.
- Ask the groups of children to decide how they will record their predictions, e.g. drawings, in a chart, on a clipboard or by drawing with chalk on the ground.
- Give each group a magnet to test their predictions and also to explore and record what they find out about a range of other places in the outdoor area.
- Call the children back after 5–10 minutes to compare their initial predictions with what they found out. Ask whether any groups had unexpected results; some may have tested metal items which were not magnetic, e.g. aluminium alloy door handles. At this point, discuss the misconception that all metals are magnetic.
- Following this, children work indoors to design and make their 'Message Magnet'. (See Design and technology cross-curricular activity.)
- When the 'Message Magnets' are complete and installed outdoors, ask children to think of questions about how they could monitor and evaluate their 'Message Magnet', e.g.: Is the magnet strong enough to hold the sign in place during strong winds?; Is the sign material weatherproof?; Does the message fade over time?

SCIENCE BACKGROUND

Magnets attract ('stick to' or 'pull') objects made from magnetic materials, e.g. iron, cobalt and nickel, which are all types of metal. It is not true that a magnet will attract *any* kind of metal. For example, aluminium alloy door handles are metal but are not usually magnetic. A magnet will not attract materials such as brick, rubber, wood, different plastics and metals such as aluminium, copper, lead and tin. Some metals (such as steel) contain iron, so a steel fence bracket will be attracted to a magnet.

A magnet is an object made of a material that creates a magnetic field around the magnet. The field gives rise to a magnetic force which has a detectable strength (i.e. 'strong' or 'weak') and direction (i.e. 'push' (repel) or 'pull' (attract)). Magnetism is a force that works at a distance. The force of magnetism is not easy to explain but, put simply, is caused by the motion of electric charges within the material. Electricity and magnetism are closely related. Michael Faraday and James Clerk Maxwell were scientists who researched early ideas about electromagnetism.

CROSS-CURRICULAR LINKS

Design and technology

Children explore a selection of commercially available fridge magnets (including some brought in from home) and evaluate how well they work. Are any too heavy for their magnet? Provide a selection of sign materials, e.g. paper, card, plastic, Corriflute, balsa wood, and types of magnets for children to choose from for their 'Message Magnet' design, e.g. button magnets, square magnets, ring magnets, magnetic strip. Children could carry out science investigations to determine the best materials to use, e.g. strongest magnet, most waterproof or light resistant marker pens, best sign material, etc. Consider a laminated 'Message Magnet' to provide weatherproofing.

When the 'Message Magnets' are complete and installed outdoors, ask children about how they could monitor and evaluate their 'Message Magnet', e.g.: Is the magnet strong enough to hold the sign in place during strong winds? Is the sign material weatherproof? Does the message fade over time? This could lead to further improvements to the 'Message Magnet' design.

Geography

Use the selection of fridge magnets and make a group of those brought back as holiday souvenirs. Children use a globe, atlas or online search to locate countries that have been visited on holidays. Extend this to carrying out a homework survey of other places that children have visited on holiday, with sensitivity to those children who may not be able to travel away for a holiday. They could report on another member of their family, e.g. grandparent, uncle or aunt, or even record where they would wish to go on holiday. Children could follow this up by researching and creating a travel brochure about a chosen holiday destination.

ACTIVITY 34
Forces flingers

Science topic
Forces – levers

Activity type
Comparative and fair testing

Resources
Elastic bands

Lolly sticks

Old rulers

Paper

Pencils

Plastic spoons

Sticky tape

Tape measures

 Safety: Remind children to check that no one is in the way when launching their missiles.

Overview
In this activity children investigate levers and forces to help them design a 'flinger' (lever catapult) which can fire paper missiles. Using the outdoor area provides children with a large, safer space in which to work.

ACTIVITY

- Prior to this activity, children research information on lever catapults such as the Roman onager and mediaeval mangonels and trebuchets for ideas to help design and make their model flinger.
- Give children a range of materials including pencils, rulers, lolly sticks, plastic spoons, elastic bands, etc. and challenge them to make a flinger that will fling a ball of paper over a distance or over an object.
- Where children have problems, encourage them to visit other groups to find out how they have built their flinger and, where appropriate, rethink and change their own design.
- Ask children to identify the lever, load and fulcrum in their design.
- Challenge the children to carry out comparative tests to improve their flinger and beat the previous distance, keeping a record of the changes and their results. Ask children to reflect on the changes they made and why they think it made a difference. Discuss what other factors might affect the distance that the missile travels, e.g. force of launch, angle of pivot, missile material, missile shape.
- Once children have carried out their comparative tests using their flinger, challenge children to formalise their tests by carrying out a 'fair test' to find out how, e.g.:

    - the length of the lever between effort (hand push down) and the pivot affects the distance that the missile travels
    - the angle affects distance travelled
    - the weight of missile affects distance travelled.

- Ask children to think about whether carrying out their fair test once creates data that is reliable. Do they need to repeat readings? Why?
- Ask the children to predict their next reading based on the pattern in results.
- Give each group the opportunity to take a photograph or video of their flinger so that once back in the classroom they can identify the fulcrum (pivot), lever, load and forces in action.

- Children could share and compare results and then create a 'super flinger' using information gained from their own and other groups' tests. How will the force be applied to operate the flinger? What safety precautions need to be considered? Which aspect that they changed do they think has had the greatest effect?

SCIENCE BACKGROUND

A lever is a simple machine. Levers have a fulcrum: the point at which the lever pivots or turns. The further the effort (or force) is from the fulcrum, the easier a load can be moved. Usually, long levers work best and can turn a small effort into a much larger one. In this lever flinger, the load is the paper ball and the fulcrum is the point at which the throwing arm pivots.

CROSS-CURRICULAR LINKS

Mathematics
This activity presents many opportunities for children to use a range of mathematics, from measuring distance and angles to taking repeat readings and calculating averages as well as working out ratio between fulcrum and force. Having collected a wide range of data, children should choose whether to transfer the data to a bar or line graph and then use the data to draw conclusions and extrapolate (estimating beyond the data on the graph) or interpolate (estimating points between data).

Design and technology
Children design their flinger, applying understanding from Science, Technology, Engineering and Mathematics (STEM) and communicating their ideas through drawings and prototypes. Then they construct their flinger using appropriate materials and construction techniques. Children evaluate their flinger against their original ideas and criteria, and against those created in, for example, Roman times. How successful is their model? Which parts work well? What could be improved?

Kites fly high

Science topic
Forces

Activity type
Comparative and fair testing

Resources
Bamboo skewers

Gloves

Plastic bin bags

Plastic carrier bags

Plastic supermarket fruit bags

Scissors

Sticky tape

Thin string

⚠ Safety: Be aware of: long strings as a tripping/strangling hazard; scissors being used outdoors; and friction burns from the string (these can be avoided by wearing gloves).

Overview
In this activity children explore the forces involved in flying kites and apply their learning to design and make a kite.

ACTIVITY

- On a breezy day, take children outside with a range of supermarket carrier bags. Begin by giving children time to explore standing, walking and running with a bag to experience the wind filling it with air and feeling the force.
- Continue exploring different kinds of bags of different sizes and materials to find out how they are similar and different.
- Children will at some point want to add string so that the bags they are using are more like traditional kites, so make sure that string and scissors are available in an area where children can go and get them.
- As children explore, take the time to wander round, asking them what changes they have made and what difference it makes to how their 'bag kite' flies and the forces they can feel. Use words such as force, pull, resistance, gravity.
- Children continue their exploration until they have created a 'bag kite' that they think flies well.
- Bring the children back together to discuss how their kites work and what changes they made. Why do they think the changes affected how well their 'bag kite' flew?
- Back in the classroom, give children time to research kites, using books, video clips and the internet. (You might want to create a folder with different files about kites that children can use.) There are many different kinds of kite such as flat kites, box kites which are three-dimensional and delta kites which are dart shaped. Give children time to research and design their kites, then they can make them and try them out.
- The next step is an important one, and that is for children to understand that scientists often try things out to establish what works well and where improvements are needed. Explain to children that they will have time to explore how their kite flies and to think about what might affect how well a kite flies, e.g. shape, weight, size, type of material and special additions to the kite such as a tail. Ask children to consider whether changing the colour or adding decorations would have any effect.
- During the process of making their kites give children the freedom to keep going outdoors to test their kites and make changes according to their experience.

- Recording their work could include photographs with comments, diagrams, and video clips with voice-over.
- When all kites have been made, hold a 'Kite Festival'. This could be as a demonstration to other year groups, the whole school and families.

SCIENCE BACKGROUND

Wind is air that is moving from one place to another. A flying kite experiences several different forces. Thrust is created when the wind blows; how fast the air moves (velocity) has an effect on how well the kite flies. Lift is a force that pushes the kite upwards because the air moves more slowly over the face of the kite and across the back more quickly, reducing pressure so the kite moves upwards. The kite also experiences the force of drag (air resistance) and the force of gravity pulls the kite downwards as does the force of the pull by the string. A kite will only fly if the overall upward force is greater than the overall downward force.

As part of science, children should develop an understanding of the difference between hazard and risk. A hazard is something that might happen, such as running into someone while looking back at the kite, long strings (tripping/strangling hazard) and friction burns from string being pulled through the hands. The risk is how likely these are to happen. In this set of activities there are many hazards but the risk of them happening depends on how sensibly the children work.

CROSS-CURRICULAR LINKS

Mathematics
Children apply a range of mathematical understanding and skills when making a kite, from measuring the dimensions of the kite and timing how long it remains in flight to using symmetry and 2D/3D shapes in designing their kite. Their designs might be based on historical and geographical research into kites from around the

world including Chinese, Japanese and Indian fighting kites. Discuss 'symmetry' with the children; why do they think a kite might need to have symmetry and why is it important for the kite to be balanced?

Design and technology

The process of testing and evaluation in science and design and technology is similar. Children engage in the design process applying understanding of forces and materials, alongside design and technology skills, and research about different kinds of kites. Then they make and test their kites, continually refining and redesigning them using information and experiences from their tests. Finally, they evaluate their kite against their original criteria, e.g. the kite has to stay in the air for a set amount of time, be able to move in a particular way and look like, for example, a Japanese carp kite.

Online resources

www.instructables.com/id/Easy-Paper-Kite-for-Kids/

ACTIVITY 36
Land yachts ahoy!

Science topic
Forces

Activity type
Fair and comparative testing

Resources
Test vehicles with a mast to attach test sails e.g. an old roller skate or vehicles that the children have constructed from construction kits such as K'NEX®, Lego® or balsa wood

Measuring tapes

Pencils

Rulers

Sail materials e.g. variety of paper, plastic and fabrics

Scissors

Sticky tape

Stopwatches

Overview
Children research, design and make a land yacht, which is a wind-powered land vehicle. Children then investigate how different sail designs affect the movement of a land yacht, collecting data to inform improvements made to create a 'super land yacht'.

ACTIVITY

- Prior to the outdoor activity, children carry out research on land yachts, finding out about the arrangement of wheels, shape and size of the sails, the body shape, etc. Then they construct their own land yacht body as a design and technology activity. Encourage children to use, for example, roller skates, skateboards and construction kits, as well as recycling everyday materials.
- Be prepared also to give children time outdoors to explore and change their prototypes. As children work, ask them questions such as the ones below to describe and explain their ideas. You could begin questions with the phrase 'I wonder …

  - … why you have used that shape?'
  - … how the materials used will affect how the land yacht moves?'
  - … how will you test your land yacht?'
  - … what variables will you change and keep the same?'
  - … what makes a super land yacht?'

- Continue to ask questions such as:

  - How does the sail affect the distance the land yacht travels and its speed?
  - What could you change about the sail? (For example, shape, material, size, position.)
  - What will you measure and how will you record your results?
  - Where will you set up a test track for the land yacht, taking the wind direction and surface into account?
  - What have you learned from your tests and the tests that others have carried out? How will you use those results to improve your land yacht?

SCIENCE BACKGROUND

Wind is air that is moving from one place to another. A land yacht experiences several different forces. The land yacht will only move if the force exerted by the wind is greater than forces resisting movement such as air resistance, friction of the wheels on the ground, and friction of moving parts within the land yacht. The force of gravity pulls the land yacht downwards. Larger sails experience more force from the wind but also have higher air resistance.

CROSS-CURRICULAR LINKS

English

Children create a marketing leaflet to advertise their land yacht or a class land yacht racing event. This could include digital photographs with captions explaining results, forces and key features. Challenge children to use a variety of persuasive literary devices.

Design and technology

Children research, design, make and test land yachts using scientific enquiry fair tests. In their land yacht design, children should use their subject knowledge about forces to reduce the effects of unwanted friction and make the best use of the force of moving air – wind. The process of testing and evaluation in science and design and technology is similar; children engage in the design process applying understanding of forces and materials, alongside design and technology skills, and research different kinds of land yachts. They then make and test their land yachts, continually refining and redesigning them using information and experiences from their tests. Finally they evaluate their land yacht against their original criteria. The project could culminate in a land yacht Grand Prix event where groups of children race their land yachts.

ACTIVITY 37
Skateboarding scientists

Science topic
Forces – gravity, friction, air resistance

Activity type
Comparative and fair testing

Resources
Measuring equipment such as tape measures and timers

Newton meters

Safety kit for children using skateboards, such as helmets, knee and elbow pads

Skateboards

Overview
This is an activity where children can apply their understanding of materials and forces to explore the science of a skateboard.

ACTIVITY

- Before going out into the school grounds, show children a video clip of an expert skateboarder or, even better, invite one into school to demonstrate their skills (wearing safety kit).
- Give children a skateboard per group. Their first task is to explore the skateboard (at this stage without riding it) to find out how it is made, what kind of materials are used, and why.
- Ask children to draw a large annotated diagram on the school playground that illustrates what they have found out.
- Each child then tries skateboarding (**safety kit must be worn**) while the others observe the skateboard deck (platform), trucks (axles) and wheels and what the skateboarder has to do to make the skateboard move.
- Ask children to note the forces in action and annotate their skateboard diagram with captions about the forces to explain how a skateboard and skateboarder moves.
- Next, ask children to carry out comparative tests on how the skateboard moves over different surfaces, using a Newton meter to measure the pull force required to start the skateboard moving. They might have a difficulty attaching the Newton meter; if so, this is a point where children engage in problem solving. Children record their results and conclusion alongside their annotated drawings.
- Ask the children to discuss and explain why they think some surfaces are easier to move over than others, referring to ideas about friction.

SCIENCE BACKGROUND

A skateboard is made up of three main components: a deck (a platform), trucks (axles) and wheels. There are a number of forces to consider such as gravity, air resistance and friction. The speed at which a skateboard travels may be affected by different forces such as friction acting on the wheels and air resistance on the body. Friction can be good for skateboarders, e.g. grips on shoes to stop them from slipping on the deck and the wheels gripping the ground when cornering. The weight of the skateboarder increases friction on the axles and between the wheels and the ground which can make the skateboard slower.

CROSS-CURRICULAR LINKS

Design and technology
Use science results to design, build and test a working skateboard that is the right size for a soft toy which could be named 'Ollie'. Some children may recognise the term 'Ollie' as a type of skateboarding jump. (The ollie is a skateboarding trick where the rider and board leap into the air.) Consider the appearance and the functions of wheels, axles and platform. Alternatively, design and build a small skateboard park with different surfaces on which 'Ollie' the toy can perform his skateboard tricks.

Computing
Ask the children to find logos on products at home, at school and on clothing. What do they think makes a good logo? Use graphics software to design a new skateboard logo for 'Ollie' the toy. Children explore the effect of using different fonts, colours and backgrounds to create the logo. Part-way through this process, give children time to ask another group to provide a critique of their draft logo, indicating what they think is successful and making suggestions for possible improvements.

Splashdown!

Science topic
Forces – gravity, air resistance, water resistance

Activity type
Comparative and fair testing

Resources
Container, e.g. bucket, filled to brim with water

Measuring equipment, e.g. metre rule, measuring cylinder

Plasticine®

Video camera to film the splash

Overview
Be prepared to get wet – the Olympic Diving Championships have come to town! So the best place to carry out this set of activities is, of course, outdoors. Children design a shape from Plasticine® to find out what affects a splash in diving. This activity is designed to encourage creativity and lateral thinking as children decide the best way to measure and record observations.

ACTIVITY

- Explain to children that in Olympic diving, the best dives have a small splash.
- In the Olympic Diving Championships, the aim is to find out what affects the splash.

- Remind the children how to plan and carry out a fair test, identifying variables that may affect the size of the splash, e.g. amount of Plasticine®, shape of diver, height of drop, method of drop, etc.
- Ask them to suggest possible investigations, changing only one variable at a time; for example, if the shape of the diver is changed, the other variables should be kept the same.
- Challenge children to think about what could be observed or measured, e.g. height of splash, volume of water displaced, area of splash, etc.
- Ask children to think about whether they need to repeat the test to ensure that their data is reliable.
- Children carry out their investigation and, if possible, video the splash.
- Children use their results to draw their conclusions. What has the greatest effect on the size of the splash? What evidence do they have to prove this?
- Which is the best shape for making the smallest splash? Which shape wins the Olympic Diving Championships? Can the children explain why?

SCIENCE BACKGROUND

There are several forces to think about here. Unsupported objects fall towards Earth because of the force of gravity. Air resistance acts on the model diver as it falls through the air. When the diver enters the water, it experiences water resistance. The splash is a disturbance caused by a solid object suddenly hitting the surface and transferring some of its energy to the water. Water is displaced by the object (diver) in the container. The more streamlined a shape is, the less resistance it has as it enters the water and the smaller the splash. Show children video clips of diving championships to illustrate an application of this idea.

CROSS-CURRICULAR LINKS

Mathematics
One of the challenges is for children to decide how to measure the splash, e.g. volume of water before and after the splash, or area of splash outside the container. Repeat readings will be one element of the tests so the average (mean) of the results can be calculated and a bar graph of the mean results for each shape used.

English
Splash is an onomatopoeic word; it imitates the sounds associated with the action that it refers to. Collect other onomatopoeic words and use some of them to 'paint a word picture' with words and sounds in a poem. Shape poems work well and can be used to make a great wall display. Children could create a cartoon of their 'Plasticine® diver' in action and, as in many cartoons, surround the images with onomatopoeic words such as splash, wham, splat.

Waterproof roof

Science topic
Uses of materials – waterproofing

Scientific enquiry
Comparative and fair testing

Resources
Lego® house

Water sprayer

Paper towels

To go large:

Long twigs/willow for walls

Optional mud for 'daub'

Overview
In this activity children test a range of natural materials found in the school grounds to decide which would make the best roof for a model house.

ACTIVITY

- The context for this activity could be, for example, history where children replicate a model Iron Age dwelling. Alternatively, the context could be a story such as 'Three Little Pigs'.

- Ask groups of children to build a Lego® house without a roof.
- Once the houses have been made, children search the school grounds for possible natural roofing materials and choose one material to build the roof for their house, e.g. leaves or twigs.
- Encourage the groups to share their roof design with the class.
- Ask the children to predict which roof they think would be the most effective; ask them to discuss within their group why one might be better than others.
- They will have to decide how to test their roof and discuss water container types to simulate rain, e.g. syringes, capacity containers, watering cans.
- For some children a comparative test might be appropriate where they compare whether or not the floor of the hut gets wet.
- More able children should decide what needs to be controlled to make a fairer test (e.g. no gaps, thickness of roof, amount of water). Challenge children to think about what and how to measure and record the moisture that gets through.

SCIENCE BACKROUND

Different materials have different properties, which make them useful for different purposes. Water cannot penetrate waterproof materials. Many materials are water-resistant – i.e. water will not soak through right away but after a while will begin to seep through. Natural materials often have a waxy coating which is water-resistant.

CROSS-CURRICULAR LINKS

History

This activity links well with a 'houses and homes' topic or a historical study of houses, e.g. Iron Age Celts and their round houses. Typically, round houses were made of wattle and daub. The wattle was made by weaving pliable wood, such as hazel or willow, to form a circular lattice wall structure. The daub, made from materials such as clay mixed with straw and dung, was applied in a sticky layer over the wattle and then dried. These walls were very good at keeping the heat in and the wind out. The roofs of the round houses were often made from materials such as heather and straw.

Design and technology

Go large! Collect twigs or use willow and insert into the ground vertically in a circle to construct a frame, then weave other twigs in and out to construct a wall. This house could be big enough for two or three children or dolls to sit inside. The roof is added using the 'best' material from the investigation. A central pole may be needed to support the roof. To take things a step further, a mud/grass mixture could be applied to create wattle and daub walls.

Online resources

http://resourcesforhistory.com/Celtic_round_houses.htm

www.bbc.co.uk/wales/celts/factfile/homes.shtml

Bubble-ology

Science topic
Materials

Activity type
Comparative and fair testing

Resources
Commercial bubble solutions

Glycerine

Liquid detergents, e.g. different brands of washing-up liquids

Lots of pots, e.g. recycled yoghurt pots for mixing solutions

Measuring equipment, e.g. teaspoons, jugs, measuring cylinders and beakers

Objects to make bubbles, e.g. plastic bottles, kitchen whisks, plastic spoons, colanders, straws, tea strainers, etc.

Pipe cleaners

Stopwatches

Supply of water

A good bubble mix is 1/2 cup(s) of washing-up liquid, 5 cups of water, 2 tablespoons of glycerine (available at the pharmacy or supermarket). Mix (don't whisk) the ingredients carefully. If possible, leave overnight.

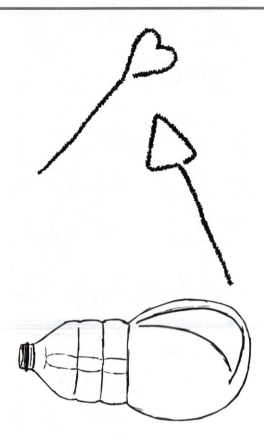

Overview

Everybody loves bubbles and they provide a huge variety of possibilities for investigations for all ages. Children can become experts in bubbles; they could even make up a name for a bubbles scientist, e.g. a 'bubbleologist'.

ACTIVITY

- Consider, as a class, how many different ways in which children can make bubbles. They could use kitchen whisks in tubs of bubble liquid, shaking bottles half-filled with bubble mixture, etc.
- Make different-shaped bubble blowers using pipe cleaners, e.g. 2D shapes like stars, squares, triangles, or 3D shapes such as pyramids and cubes.
- What do the children notice about the bubbles? What happens when bubbles touch? Can bubbles be joined together? How? How can children blow bubbles inside bubbles?
- Children could carry out fair tests to find out which is the best recipe for bubble solutions using different types of washing-up liquid, or test which is the best ratio of water to washing-up liquid for bubble making.
- Children could set up their own enterprise making and selling their bubble mixture, working out how much it costs to make the mixture, containers and what they should sell the mixture for to make a profit. The profit could be used to purchase a special piece of science equipment or be donated to a local charity.
- Finally, children could practise stunt bubbles – e.g. long bubbles, bubbles in bubbles, bubbles rolling up and down string – to demonstrate to younger year groups.

SCIENCE BACKGROUND

By itself water does not make good bubbles, but adding detergent changes the surface tension. Surface tension is a property of water that causes it to behave as if its surface were covered with a stretchy 'skin' because of invisible bonds that hold the water molecules together. Adding the detergent allows this 'skin' to become more elastic (stretchy). Then it can be more like the skin of a balloon, stretching out and trapping air inside the bubble. Surface tension is the reason why bubbles are round because this is the shape that has the smallest surface area for a particular amount of air trapped inside. If you keep blowing more air in, the 'skin' gets thinner as it stretches and eventually the bubble bursts. Bubbles are always round and they like to be wet. If you put something dry against a bubble it will burst; wet a plastic straw and it can be placed inside a bubble. Bubbles reflect the colours in the environment and children will also see the colours of rainbows in a bubble, so they could memorise a mnemonic to learn the order of the colours of the rainbow (red, orange, yellow, green, blue, indigo, violet), e.g. **R**ichard **O**f **Y**ork **G**ave **B**attle **I**n **V**ain. Alternatively, they can create their own.

CROSS-CURRICULAR LINKS

Art
Here are several ideas for how to create some bubble-inspired artwork. Add washing-up liquid to ready-mixed paint and use straws to blow bubbles. Place paper over the paint bubbles to make bubble prints. Alternatively, study rainbows and colours on soap bubbles and use wet-on-wet watercolour washes to recreate some of the patterns and colours observed. Children could create 'doodle art' using only bubble shapes with fine black or different coloured pens. Using chalks on black paper, children could sketch bubbles focusing on their shape and colours in reflections. Kitchen towel tubes or other cylindrical objects could be used to print circles and create bubble shapes. Children could wrap 'bubble wrap' around their feet so that they can walk through a paint tray and 'bubble wrap' walk over long strips of paper, e.g. backing paper for wallpaper.

English
The beauty of bubbles can inspire children to write stunning poetry. Haiku poetry works particularly well, especially if a simile is included, or a shape poem could fit neatly into a bubble. Children could use background designs created by a variety of art techniques and write their poem on top of these. They could also create a cover for a 'bubbleology' book, explaining the science of bubbles.

Online resources
www.sciencemuseum.org.uk/visitmuseum/Plan_your_visit/events/science_shows/bubbles_bubbles_bubbles/making_perfect_bubbles.aspx

Magic potion

Science topic
Materials – chemical change

Activity type
Observation over time

Resources
500g of Bicarbonate of soda (sodium bicarbonate)

Bottle of vinegar

1 can of shaving foam

Optional food colouring

Spray bottles e.g. plant sprayer

Safety goggles

 Safety: Children should wear safety goggles when using vinegar.

Overview
In this activity children make foam 'snowballs', then add a 'magic potion' and observe the effects; this is definitely an outdoors activity as the result can be quite messy and pungent!

ACTIVITY

- The first step is to make the foam 'snow'. This can be a whole class activity or a group activity using smaller amounts of ingredients. Put the sodium bicarbonate in a large bowl then mix in the shaving foam; start with about half the can then gradually add more to give a thick snow-like consistency. You could use a spoon, but using fingers is more fun!
- Children take a small handful of the 'snow' and form it into a ball; then they place their 'snowball' into a small bowl.
- At this stage because children will be using vinegar they should wear safety goggles to protect their eyes.
- Each group is given a spray bottle (e.g. plant sprayer) full of 'magic potion' which is, in fact, vinegar. Ask children to predict what will happen if some of the 'magic potion' is added.
- Children should be ready to video or photograph the chemical reaction.
- The children spray a little vinegar onto the 'snowballs' and observe what happens. It will fizz and bubble on the surface. Back in the classroom, review the video or photographs and discuss what kind of changes took place.
- Ask the children to think about cause and effect and whether they think the change could be reversed. Challenge children to use specific scientific vocabulary, e.g. reaction, change, cause, effect, vinegar, bicarbonate of soda, gas, carbon dioxide.

SCIENCE BACKGROUND

The chemical reaction between sodium bicarbonate and vinegar generates bubbles of carbon dioxide gas which cause the fizzing. A chemical reaction is a process that changes one set of chemical substances to another. Initially, the carbon dioxide gas bubbles are trapped within the foam, which makes it expand, but eventually the gas will escape into the air. This chemical change is irreversible.

CROSS–CURRICULAR LINKS

English

Children write an instructional text including imperative verbs to help other children to make their own magic potion snowballs. They should use appropriate devices to structure their writing (e.g. headings, lists and bullet points) and appropriate punctuation (such as a colon to introduce a list, and consistency with punctuation of bullet points). The instructions could also include an explanation of what happens during the chemical reaction when the fizzing occurs. A word bank of key scientific vocabulary could be provided, e.g. reaction, change, cause, effect, vinegar, bicarbonate of soda, gas, carbon dioxide, reversible and irreversible.

Music

Ask the children to use a microphone to record the fizzing sound produced when the bubbles of carbon dioxide are being formed and listen carefully to the recording, describing what can be heard. Encourage children to use musical vocabulary, e.g. pitch, duration, dynamics, tempo, timbre, etc. The children could listen to the instrumental song 'Popcorn' by Hot Butter and appraise the music in the same way. This may extend to a musical composition either using conventional instruments or computer software.

Awesome snowflakes

Science topic
Materials – changes of state, melting

Activity type
Observing over time

Resources
Containers, e.g. Petri dishes

Individual whiteboards and markers

Microscopes (portable digital or traditional optical) – one indoors and one outdoors

Teaspoons

Overview
This is an activity which, of course, can only be carried out when it is snowing. It provides an opportunity for children to observe snowflakes using a microscope, so it will be important to make sure that children have had experience of using a microscope first.

ACTIVITY

- Show the children the equipment available and ask them to think about how they are going to find out what snowflakes look like using the microscope. Discuss with children what would happen if they used 'warm' resources straight from the classroom, so that they understand that they will have to leave equipment outside for a while so that it can cool to the outdoor temperature.

- Children could use a thermometer or data logger to measure the air temperature indoors and compare it to the temperature of the air outdoors. What do they notice? What is the temperature of the snow?
- Ask the children to think about how they are going to look at snowflakes using the microscope. One of the easiest ways is to use a teaspoon to put a little snow into a shallow transparent container, e.g. a Petri dish.
- Prompt children to think about how to hold containers, because cradling the container in warm hands may cause the snow to melt immediately.
- Ask children to write descriptive words on an individual whiteboard, or go around and record words for them.
- If using a remote digital microscope, use the image capture facility to photograph the snow or ice crystals.
- As children observe the snow and ice how does it change?
- Children could take a ball of snow or ice into the classroom and observe changes over a short period of time. What changes have occurred? How might the air temperature have affected this? Children could measure the temperature of the air and the water during the rest of the day and should find that the water warms to room temperature.

SCIENCE BACKGROUND

Melting is the physical process which occurs when a solid (e.g. snow or ice) changes to a liquid state. Bringing the snow indoors results in warming of the snow above 0°C, its melting point, as room temperature is typically around 20°C. Some of the heat energy in the room transfers to the snow, it melts and then the resulting liquid (water) eventually warms to room temperature.

CROSS-CURRICULAR LINKS

English

Engage children in creative writing – for example, a piece entitled 'Snowflake's Adventure'. Ask them to imagine a snowflake living happily in its cold environment but wanting to explore the world. Children use descriptive words from the outdoor activity to write a story or poem about the snowflake's adventures as it travels. An event could take place which sadly causes the snowflake to melt. What do they think that event might be?

Geography

Ask children to research which countries do and do not have snowfall and where in the world snow stays all year round. How might this affect the lives of people living in these places? Where in the world has the heaviest snowfall been recorded? Identify seasonal weather patterns in the United Kingdom and the location of cold areas of the world in relation to the Equator and the North and South Poles. Children could place this information as captions around a world map.

Texture trail

Science topics
Everyday materials; Physical properties relating to texture

Activity type
Identifying, classifying and grouping

Resources
A4 paper

Chalk or wax crayons

Overview
Children explore materials outdoors – both natural and made. Some children may need to be taught or reminded of how to take rubbings of different surfaces.

ACTIVITY

- Children search for different materials in the outdoor area.
- How many different materials (e.g. brick, stone, wood, plastic, glass, metal) can they identify and name?
- Ask children to carefully touch the surfaces (care with glass) and describe how each one feels, e.g. rough, smooth, cold and warm.
- If necessary, demonstrate how to hold paper firmly in place over the material and rub over with a wax crayon or chalk to create a rubbing of the surface's texture.
- Emphasise that the colour of the rubbing isn't important but the pattern created by the texture is.
- Each group makes rubbings of three different surfaces.

- Lay the paper out on the yard. Ask children to describe what the textures look like to develop vocabulary. Challenge children to group together similar textures.
- You could say: 'I wonder how we could use our rubbings to create a "texture trail" around the school grounds which other children could use at playtimes and by other classes when they learn about materials.'
- After discussions, children choose the best idea, create a school texture trail and then teach other children how to use it.

SCIENCE BACKGROUND

Texture is the tactile quality of a surface and is related to physical properties of the material. Texture tells us about the appearance and feel of a surface – e.g. the smooth texture of a bar of soap – and is an important characteristic of the material. A material may have different textures depending on how it has been formed or processed, e.g. hard, rough rocks can be polished to have a hard, smooth surface.

CROSS-CURRICULAR LINKS

Art
Children could use squares of paper the same size and create different rubbings, e.g. different textures of tree bark, bricks etc. Encourage children to explore using different pressure and colours to create different effects. They could then arrange their squares to create a pattern by placing the squares in different positions, rather like a quilt.

Physical education (dance)
Children can explore movement to interpret different texture stimulus words, e.g. dimpled, fluffy, gritty, hard, leathery, lumpy, prickly, rough, slippery, smooth, soft, spongy and velvety. This could be developed into a structured group dance composition using a series of two or three repeated contrasting textures (movements) to perform outdoors at positions around the texture trail.

Peek-a-boo toys

Science topic
Properties of materials – absorbency

Activity type
Comparative and fair testing

Resources
Bowls or tray

Camera

Chalk

Different types of paper and card

Rulers

Scissors

Small plastic toys

Stopwatches

Water

Overview

Children make folded paper flowers to float on water and investigate how quickly the flowers unfold. Working outside not only means less mess but also gives more space so that all children can carry out this activity using a range of containers, including bowls, trays and ice-cream tubs.

ACTIVITY

- Prior to going outside, children make a large paper flower shape and fold each petal to the centre. They choose a small, lightweight toy – e.g. plastic dinosaur or Lego® person – to place inside the folded paper. Alternatively, children could draw a picture in the centre of the flower before folding the petals in.
- Once outside children float the closed flower on the water in either a water tray or a plastic bowl.
- Children observe their flower as the petals open and the toy is revealed. You could say to the children: 'I wonder why that happened? What do you think?'
- Children get quite excited and will want to make other flowers, so do let them try out their ideas and explore, for example,

different paper, card, newspaper, etc. Materials could be brought outside so that the children can make as well as test their flowers outdoors.

- Some children could be challenged to move from a simple comparative test, where they just try something out and observe to thinking about what to change and how to keep it fair.
- Ask the children to think about how they will measure the time each flower takes to open. Flowers made from different types of paper could be floated at the same time to compare which opens first, or floated separately and timed to measure how long they take to open.
- Ask the children to think about what else they could investigate, e.g. different size flowers, weight of different toys, different paper textures, card versus paper, etc.

SCIENCE BACKGROUND

Paper is made from fibres which can absorb water and swell. The paper surface in contact with the water expands, causing the flower petals to open. Different papers have different types of fibres and so absorb water at different rates. This means that the time taken for the flower to open is different too.

CROSS-CURRICULAR LINKS

Mathematics
Children will need to develop a range of measuring skills to create accurate flower sizes.

Children might need to be taught or reminded of how to use a stopwatch, so they know how to:

- start it at the right time
- have a signal to stop the watch when they think the flower is fully open
- record in a table and reset the timer for the next flower.

The results of the investigation can be recorded in a bar graph. This could be constructed on the playground using chalks to draw the axes. Don't forget to have a camera handy so that children can take photographs as a record of their activity and of the finished playground graph.

Languages

The investigation provides an opportunity for children to communicate using the foreign language that they are learning at school. For example, the person placing the flower on the water may say 'Start', at the beginning and 'Stop' or 'The flower has opened' as a signal to their friend to stop the stopwatch. Children could use an online translation website to find out the required phrases and their pronunciation.

Taylor & Francis eBooks

Helping you to choose the right eBooks for your Library

Add Routledge titles to your library's digital collection today. Taylor and Francis ebooks contains over 50,000 titles in the Humanities, Social Sciences, Behavioural Sciences, Built Environment and Law.

Choose from a range of subject packages or create your own!

Benefits for you

» Free MARC records
» COUNTER-compliant usage statistics
» Flexible purchase and pricing options
» All titles DRM-free.

REQUEST YOUR FREE INSTITUTIONAL TRIAL TODAY
Free Trials Available
We offer free trials to qualifying academic, corporate and government customers.

Benefits for your user

» Off-site, anytime access via Athens or referring URL
» Print or copy pages or chapters
» Full content search
» Bookmark, highlight and annotate text
» Access to thousands of pages of quality research at the click of a button.

eCollections – Choose from over 30 subject eCollections, including:

Archaeology	Language Learning
Architecture	Law
Asian Studies	Literature
Business & Management	Media & Communication
Classical Studies	Middle East Studies
Construction	Music
Creative & Media Arts	Philosophy
Criminology & Criminal Justice	Planning
Economics	Politics
Education	Psychology & Mental Health
Energy	Religion
Engineering	Security
English Language & Linguistics	Social Work
Environment & Sustainability	Sociology
Geography	Sport
Health Studies	Theatre & Performance
History	Tourism, Hospitality & Events

For more information, pricing enquiries or to order a free trial, please contact your local sales team: www.tandfebooks.com/page/sales

Routledge
Taylor & Francis Group | The home of Routledge books

www.tandfebooks.com

Get ready to...

Jumpstart!

The *Jumpstart!* books contain 'quick-figure' ideas that could be used as warm-ups and starters as well as possibly extended into lessons. There are more than 50 games and activities for Key Stage 1 or 2 classrooms that are practical, easy-to-do and vastly entertaining.

To find out more about other books in the Jumpstart! series, or to order online, please visit:

www.routledge.com/u/jumpstart/